W9-CEW-407

OF THE

AFRICAN AMERICAN CIVIL RIGHTS MOVEMENT

to sit down together at the table of brotherhood.... I have a dream that my four little children will one day live in a nation where they will not be judged by the color of their skin but by the content of their character.... I have a dream that one day little black boys and black girls will be able to join hands with little white boys and white girls and walk together as sisters and brothers."

When Martin Luther King spoke, black people had been living in the United States for nearly 350 years. For the first 250 years most of them had been slaves in the South. Slavery came to an end during the course of the terrible Civil War, nearly 100 years before King's speech. In the years after the war, however, blacks continued to suffer brutal oppression. Starting in the early decades of the twentieth century, thousands of blacks moved from the rural South to northern cities in search of economic opportunity. There, too, they had to put up with poverty and racial prejudice.

In the early 1900s, however, blacks and sympathetic white people started a movement to achieve full political, economic, and social equality for blacks. This was the civil rights movement. It continued to gather strength and on that hot August day in 1963, the Reverend Martin Luther King, Jr., stood at its head. The movement changed the U.S. The causes and consequences of the American civil rights movement create a colorful, and at times heartbreaking, story.

Attitudes towards slavery in the North and South differed greatly, causing many years of conflict. This cartoon of 1856 was published under the title of Disunited States, a Black Business. *It accurately predicted the approaching struggle over the issue of slavery.*

SLAVERY IN AMERICA

We hold these truths to be self-evident, that all men are created equal, that they are endowed by their Creator with certain unalienable Rights, that among these rights are Life, Liberty, and the pursuit of Happiness.

Declaration of Independence, 1776.

I was soon put down under the decks, and there . . . with the loathsomeness of the stench, and crying together, I became so sick and low that I was not able to eat, nor had I the least desire to taste any thing. I now wished for the last friend, death, to relieve me . . . . The crew used to watch us very closely who were not chained down to the decks, lest we should leap into the water; and I have seen some of the poor African prisoners, most severely cut for attempting to do so.

From The Interesting Narrative of the Life of Olaudah Equiano, or Gustavus Vasa, the African, Written by Himself *(London, 1789).*

The great-grandparents of Martin Luther King were slaves — people owned as property by other people. Other, earlier black leaders were the children of slaves or had been slaves themselves. Most of the black people in the U.S. today are descendants of slaves. Blacks' experience of slavery and slavery's legacy of oppression and prejudice were among the fundamental causes of the American civil rights movement.

George Washington, the "father of his country," owned slaves; so did Patrick Henry, who demanded in the early days of the American Revolution, "Give me liberty or give me death"; so did Thomas Jefferson, the author of the Declaration of Independence. Eight of the first 12 presidents owned slaves. The U.S., a country founded on the ideals of equality and liberty, has had black slavery closely interwoven in its history from the earliest days of its existence.

SLAVERY COMES TO AMERICA

The first blacks in America came from Africa. The international slave trade was established in the late fifteenth century, when Portuguese merchants began trading with West Africa. Slavery already existed among the Africans themselves. First the Portuguese and then other European merchants established fortresses on the West African coast in order to trade with local African rulers. Slaves were one of the "goods" that were exchanged.

The slave trade soon became a highly profitable business. By the 1700s, British and French traders had established a network of contacts that allowed them to reach beyond the coast. Local chiefs from the African interior would round up men, women, and children and then bring them to the European traders on the coast to be sold into slavery. Initially, slaves were sold in Greece, Turkey, or Eastern Europe. Later on, the trade was dominated by the New World.

CAUSES AND CONSEQUENCES

OF THE

AFRICAN AMERICAN CIVIL RIGHTS MOVEMENT

MICHAEL WEBER

RSVP

RAINTREE
STECK-VAUGHN
PUBLISHERS
The Steck-Vaughn Company

Austin, Texas

Published by Raintree Steck-Vaughn Publishers, an imprint of Steck-Vaughn Company

Developed by the Creative Publishing Company
Editor: Helena Ramsay
Designed by Ian Winton

Raintree Steck-Vaughn Publishers staff
Project Manager: Lyda Guz
Editors: Shirley Shalit, Pam Wells
Electronic Production: Scott Melcer

Consultants: Andrew Frank, University of Florida
Michael MacCarthy Morrogh, Shrewsbury School

Cover photo (large): Civil rights marchers during March on Washington, D.C., August 1963. Marchers pass the Washington Monument.
Cover photo (small): A restaurant in Maryland has a sign that reads "This Door White Only." African Americans were supposed to use the rear entrance. Photo was taken in 1948.

Library of Congress Cataloging-in-Publication Data

Weber, Michael, 1945–
    Causes and consequences of the African American civil rights movement / Michael Weber.
        p.   cm. — (Causes and consequences)
    Includes bibliographical references and index.
    Summary: Discusses the causes and consequences of the movement to achieve full political, economic, and social equality for blacks.
    ISBN 0-8172-4058-6
    1. Afro-Americans — Civil rights — History — 20th century — Juvenile literature.   2. Civil rights movement — United States — History — 20th century — Juvenile literature.   3. United States — Race relations — Juvenile literature.   [1. Afro-Americans — Civil rights.   2. Civil rights movement   3. Race relations.]   I. Title.   II. Series.
E185.61.W37   1998
323.1'196073—dc21   97-37361
                                                                 CIP   AC

Printed in Hong Kong
Bound in the United States
1 2 3 4 5 6 7 8 9 0 LB 01 00 99 98 97

CONTENTS

INTRODUCTION

On the hot, sunny afternoon of August 28, 1963, a black Baptist preacher from Montgomery, Alabama, named the Reverend Martin Luther King, Jr., stood on the steps of the Lincoln Memorial in Washington, D.C. Before him was an intense crowd, probably more than 250,000 people. To this audience — blacks and whites, young and old, men and women — King delivered one of the most moving speeches in all of American history:

"I say to you today, my friends, that in spite of the difficulties and frustrations of the moment I still have a dream. It is a dream deeply rooted in the American dream.

"I have a dream that one day...the sons of former slaves and the sons of former slave owners will be able

Martin Luther King, Jr., greets some of the 250,000 participants at the 1963 Civil Rights March on Washington, D.C. The rally provided an opportunity for black civil rights leaders to tell the nation about the racist attitudes that were still dominant in the South.

The unfortunate captives were shipped in unimaginably horrible conditions. The journey to America could take several weeks or even months. Until the slave trade was abolished in the 1800s, more than 600,000 Africans were brought to North America in this way. Millions more went to the West Indies and Central and South America.

Why were Africans made slaves? Historians have debated this question over the years. Several factors appear to have been responsible. To Europeans, blacks from Africa seemed to be different from other people. Their very skin color set them apart. "Blackness" had for a long time been associated in European culture with the devil, immorality, and dirt. Many Europeans considered the Africans primitive and inferior. Furthermore, they were not Christians.

BLACKS IN THE UNITED STATES

Whatever the complex reasons, the slavery of blacks became firmly established and legally recognized in all Britain's North American colonies. As the need for agricultural labor increased in the southern colonies, the number of slaves there grew. In 1776, during the American Revolution, these colonies were combined to create the United States. In 1790, the year of the

This engraving shows slaves being loaded on to a ship for the voyage to the Americas. Many of them died from smallpox or dysentery during the journey. The survivors endured dreadful conditions. They were crammed into the ship's hull and chained to prevent them from rebelling or jumping overboard. Just enough food, air, and light were provided to keep them alive.

first United States census, there were 757,363 black people in the country, 19 percent of the total population. Of these blacks, 697,897 were slaves, and 94 percent of the slaves were in the South. By 1860, shortly before the Civil War began, there were 4,441,830 blacks in the United States. This was 14 percent of the total population. Nearly four million were slaves, virtually all in the South. Throughout the United States, blacks, whether slave or free, suffered bitterly from discrimination and prejudice.

It is probably impossible for us to understand fully the misery of slavery. Slaves were property. They had virtually no rights under the law. The point of their existence was to work for their owners. Most were given little or no education. The conditions of their work, their rewards and punishments, their food, shelter, and housing — all were at the whim of their owners. Slaves could be bought and sold repeatedly. One of the cruelest aspects of slavery was that families of slaves — husband and wife, parents and children — could be broken up if an owner decided to sell individual family members.

In both the North and the South, even free blacks suffered greatly from discrimination. Conditions varied from time to time and state to state, but blacks generally had to endure numerous restrictions of their rights. For example, their right to schooling was often limited, as was their right to choose where they worked and whom they married. Most important of all, their right to vote was often severely restricted. The denial of these and other fundamental liberties drove blacks to live on the margins of society.

The ideals of freedom and liberty for which the American Revolution was fought between 1775–1783 led to attempts to end slavery. Several northern states ended slavery around the time of the Revolution or

This is a picture of a sugar plantation in the mid-nineteenth century. Notice the whipping taking place in the background. Punishments of this kind were all too common. One slave owner is said to have put unsatisfactory workers into a barrel with nails driven into it and then rolled the barrel down a hill.

not long afterward. The Northwest Ordinance of 1787 barred slavery from the territory that would later become the states of Ohio, Indiana, Illinois, Michigan, and Wisconsin. Many early American leaders believed slavery was truly a great evil. Some, however, including Jefferson, thought blacks inferior to whites and doubted that the two races could live together peacefully. They gave consideration to removing the black population from the U.S. to Africa or some other distant place. But no practical way of doing this was ever devised.

THE NORTH-SOUTH DIVIDE

In 1787, slavery was both recognized by and protected in the United States Constitution. The southern delegates who attended the convention at which the Constitution was written made sure of this. This constitutional protection continued to be given to the slave trade for 20 years. After this, it was possible to abolish the trade through legislative action. However, in the South the invention of the cotton gin in 1793 made slave labor even more important. Slaves were needed to operate the gins, which made it much easier and quicker to separate the valuable cotton fiber from the worthless seeds. As a result, cotton plantations became more profitable, and fewer and fewer Southerners looked favorably on the abolition of slavery.

Eli Whitney of Massachusetts invented the first cotton gin in 1793. The machine, which was simple enough for any worker to operate, consisted of a series of bristles, rollers, and hooks that separated the seeds from the cotton fiber.

Many in the South once believed that slavery was moral and political evil. That folly and delusion are now gone. We see it now in its true light, and regard it as the most safe and stable basis for free institutions in the world.

John C. Calhoun of South Carolina, 1838.

11

Many slaves attempted to escape. Federal Fugitive Slave Laws, first passed in 1793, allowed slave owners to pursue and capture runaway slaves in another state. The law also made it illegal to hide a fugitive slave or prevent his or her arrest.

As the South became almost totally dependent on slavery, North and South began to grow apart. Although only one white family in four owned any slaves, southern society and the economy that supported it were so closely linked to slavery that nobody in the South could imagine life without it. Consequently, the South became very sensitive to any movement or proposal that could be considered hostile to slavery. Leading southern thinkers developed the view that slavery, far from being a regrettable evil, was authorized by the Bible and was a positive good — for whites and blacks alike.

Some blacks did not accept their unfortunate situation quietly. Even early on, they resisted injustice. Slaves often tried to run away, and from time to time, slave rebellions did occur. The possibility of such revolts terrified the South. Free blacks in the North, where whites were more sympathetic, tried to improve their condition through petitions, court actions, and other peaceful means, and some states did lessen legal discrimination against blacks. It has been said that these acts of resistance to injustice represent the birth of the civil rights movement.

A growing sense that slavery was wrong developed in the North during the first half of the nineteenth century. Abolitionism — a movement to end slavery — gradually gathered strength. Abolitionists helped thousands of blacks to escape from southern slavery. Having made their escape they often went to the North or Canada, using a network of sympathizers known as the Underground Railroad.

The abolitionists formed only a small minority in the North. Few northerners — and not even all abolitionists — believed that blacks should have an equal place in society with whites. Nevertheless, the abolitionists frightened and infuriated the South.

SLAVERY AND THE CIVIL WAR

In the 1850s, tensions over slavery led to one crisis after another between North and South. People opposed to the spread of slavery to new areas in the United States founded a new political party, the Republican party, in 1854. Southerners accused the Republicans, incorrectly, of being abolitionists. The tension reached a climax in 1860 with the election of the Republican Abraham Lincoln as President. Eleven southern states seceded, or left, the United States and formed the Confederate States of America, or Confederacy. President Lincoln and the United States government refused to accept the legality of secession, and the Civil War began.

Slavery was the underlying cause of the Civil War. Initially, however, the war was not fought to end slavery, for the North's intention was to restore the Union as it had been before the 11 states seceded. Many Northerners — just like Southerners — were prejudiced against blacks. Lincoln himself had earlier expressed ambiguous views about the place of black people in American society.

As the war went on, attitudes began to change. The millions of slaves in the Confederacy made up almost 40 percent of its population and were the bulk of its workforce. Northern leaders realized that they could weaken the Confederacy by attacking the southern tradition of slavery. They were also aware that Britain and France were opposed to slavery. They would be more likely to support the Union if they associated the war with the abolition of slavery in the South. Moreover, as the death and destruction caused by the war mounted, the moral ideal of ending slavery began to be perceived as a worthy aim and a justification for the war.

In September 1862, Lincoln issued the Emancipation Proclamation. It said that as of January 1, 1863, all slaves in areas controlled by the Confederacy "shall be then,

Harriet Tubman (1820-1913) escaped from slavery to become one of the most famous and successful "conductors" on the Underground Railroad. She brought more than 300 slaves to safety in the North.

[Blacks are] entitled to all the natural rights enumerated in the Declaration of Independence, the right to life, liberty, and the pursuit of happiness . . . . [But] I am not, nor ever have been in favor of bringing about in any way the social and political equality of the white and black races . . . . [Still,] in the right to eat the bread, without leave of anyone else, which his own hand earns, [a black person] is my equal and the equal of . . . every living man.

Abraham Lincoln, 1858.

thenceforward, and forever free." The Proclamation inspired thousands of slaves to flee behind the lines of the Union armies. Prejudice against blacks remained, however. This was clearly shown in 1863, when terrible race riots occurred in several northern cities. White workers resented being compelled to fight to free blacks who, they thought, might then compete with them for jobs. The worst disturbances took place in New York City over four days in July. Here, the riot began as a demonstration against military conscription. The demonstration quickly descended into violence. Buildings were set on fire, shops were looted, and lynch mobs terrorized and murdered more than a hundred people, most of them blacks. Nevertheless, in 1864 Republican leaders in Congress with Lincoln's support prepared a constitutional amendment to abolish slavery everywhere in the United States. By the end of 1865, it was ratified as the Thirteenth Amendment.

The Civil War ended in April 1865 with the victory of the North over the South. But what would the victory mean for America's black people? Would the newly free slaves in the South — and all the blacks in the United States — finally become equal members of American society?

This cartoon by Thomas Nast was first published in Harper's Weekly *in 1874. It shows that less than 10 years after the Civil War ended, blacks were suffering injustice, discrimination, and persecution by whites.*

THE JIM CROW ERA

RECONSTRUCTION

After the Civil War, the emancipated slaves of the South and blacks all over the U.S. expected to become full-fledged United States citizens. They expected to be given social, political, and economic equality with white people. When they had been granted these basic civil rights, they could then expect to benefit from the nation's "new birth of freedom" that President Lincoln described as the legacy of the war. These hopes were not to be realized, and it could be said that the civil rights movement was rooted in the failure of American society to live up to the promises of emancipation.

The Civil War was followed by the Reconstruction period. This was the term used to refer to the nation's efforts to solve the political and social problems created by the war. Although there were some positive achievements for blacks during this period, Reconstruction failed to ensure equal status for all in American society. After Reconstruction ended in the 1870s, blacks in the South — who represented 90 percent of the country's African American population — fell victim to harsh new discrimination. The brutality and oppression they experienced in the late nineteenth and early twentieth centuries can be identified as another cause of the civil rights movement.

As Reconstruction began former slaves, who were known as the freedmen, were helped by a federal agency called the Freedmen's Bureau. The Bureau had been established in March 1865, while the war was still going on. It was set up to help former slaves and whites who were fleeing from areas of fighting in the South. After the war, Congress expanded the Bureau's activities. It was used to supply food and medical care to ex-slaves, to arrange work for them, and to supervise their contracts with plantation owners. The Bureau also offered to rent them land that had been confiscated from Confederates, and to set up courts and boards to settle their disputes. Finally, it also established schools and colleges, staffed largely by northerners, to educate the freedmen.

Throughout the South, blacks held meetings to call for civil rights and a fair chance to live decent lives. They protested against a series of laws passed in the South during the months immediately following the Civil War. These laws, known as the Black Codes, were passed by state governments that were dominated by former Confederates. The Black Codes denied African Americans full civil rights. Farming and servants' work were the only jobs that they were allowed to do. They could not use guns or vote and they were subject to all kinds of fines. If they did not pay the fines promptly, they could be forced to work for whites. This was not too far from slavery.

Several northern states continued to deny African Americans various civil rights, including the right to vote. Nevertheless, the Black Codes outraged many northerners. The Radical Republicans, a strong faction in Congress, were particularly incensed by the Codes. They were determined to guarantee equal rights for blacks in the South. By doing so, they also expected to win black voters, thus ensuring that they would have Republican victories in elections.

The Radical Republicans proposed measures that would protect the rights of African Americans by enhancing the powers of the federal government at the expense of the states. This conflict between federal power and the power of the state was to arise again and again during the struggle for civil rights.

Starting in spring 1866, Congress passed a series of laws to help the freedmen. These laws were passed despite the opposition of President Andrew Johnson, Lincoln's successor. The Civil Rights Act of 1866 declared that blacks were United States citizens and prohibited states from limiting their rights to testify in court or to own property. A few months later, concerned that a future Congress or the Supreme Court might undo the Civil Rights Act, Congress drafted the Fourteenth Amendment to the Constitution. This amendment defined citizenship to include African Americans and prohibited discriminatory laws like the Black Codes.

The proposed amendment could not go into effect, however, unless three-quarters of the states approved it. All the former Confederate states except Tennessee

All persons born or naturalized in the United States, and subject to the jurisdiction thereof, are citizens of the United States and of the State wherein they reside. No State shall make or enforce any law which shall abridge the privileges or immunities of citizens of the United States; nor shall any State deprive any person of life, liberty, or property, without due process of law; nor deny to any person within its jurisdiction the equal protection of the laws.

Fourteenth Amendment to the Constitution, Section 1.

rejected it. That situation and the continuing denial of African American rights in the South led to more legislation. Congress divided all of the South except for Tennessee into five military districts. It was announced that normal civilian rule would not be restored to the southern states until they altered their constitutions and ratified the Fourteenth Amendment. It took five years for Congress to decide that all the former Confederate states had met these requirements.

Under the Fourteenth Amendment, any state that denied suffrage to a proportion of its adult male citizens was penalized by a reduction in state representation at Congress. The reduction corresponded exactly to the percentage of adult males that had been denied the vote. Although this encouraged states to give African Americans the vote, it did not absolutely ensure their enfranchisement. Some southern states still found ways of refusing African Americans their voting rights. It was not until the Fifteenth Amendment was ratified in 1870 that all southern states were legally required to allow blacks to vote.

The Fourteenth Amendment did succeed at first in enfranchising many southern blacks. This illustration, published in Harper's Weekly *under the title of* The First Vote, *shows African American voters in the South during the state elections of 1867.*

General Ulysses S. Grant (1822–1885) easily defeated the Democrat Horatio Seymour in the presidential election of 1868. Grant had commanded all of the Union armies at the end of the Civil War.

Once the southern blacks were enfranchised, they voted overwhelmingly for Republicans. The approximately 450,000 votes cast by southern blacks in favor of General Ulysses S. Grant, the Republican presidential candidate in 1868, probably won him the election. In some northern states, however, African Americans were still without the vote. Republicans acted quickly to try to ensure that all blacks could vote. In early 1869, Congress proposed the Fifteenth Amendment to guarantee the right to vote to all blacks in the United States. The amendment was ratified the following year. President Grant called it "the most important event that has occurred since the nation came to life."

The right of citizens of the United States to vote shall not be denied or abridged by the United States or by any State on account of race, color, or previous condition of servitude.

Fifteenth Amendment to the Constitution.

The new state governments in the South, which were led by Republicans, made important reforms. For the first time, African Americans could freely take part in public life and hundreds of them served in state and local offices. The reform governments were often led by former northerners who had come South.

They were frequently denounced as "carpetbaggers" by their southern white opponents. This was because they were said to arrive from the North with so few possessions that they could all be fitted into a small carpetbag.

During this period, 20 blacks were elected to the House of Representatives and two to the United States Senate. The new state governments repealed the Black Codes and made a start at reviving and modernizing the region's economy. They also created the South's first public school system, which had separate schools for blacks and whites. Many southern whites bitterly mocked the new state governments in which blacks participated. They accused the blacks of being ignorant, and said the governments were corrupt, despite the fact that they were no more corrupt than other governments in the country at the time, including the national government.

THE FAILURE OF RECONSTRUCTION

When the Civil War ended, many freedmen expected to be given "forty acres and a mule" so that they could become independent farmers and support themselves. For most, this never happened. Much of the land that initially had been taken from the white slave owners was later returned to those whites. By 1880, only about 20 percent of the blacks in the South owned the land they worked. Blacks had to work for white landowners under conditions not much better than slavery. Some were paid very low wages. Others worked under arrangements whereby they leased their land in return for a share of the crops that they raised. These "sharecroppers" often ended up hopelessly in debt to the landowners for necessary farm equipment and other supplies.

Nor did political and legal gains made by blacks last long. Wealthy whites, who were usually former slave owners, united with the poor whites who bitterly resented the freedmen's gains. Together they opposed government reform and rallied support for the Democratic party in an attempt win back control. Finally, they resorted to terrorism, intimidating both blacks and whites in order to dissuade them from voting Republican.

The most notorious terrorist group was the Ku Klux Klan, or KKK. The KKK operated throughout the

Why do you take away our lands? You take them from us who have always been true, always true to the Government! You give them to our all-time enemies! That is not right!

Blacks in Georgia, protesting the return of their land to its former owners, ex-Confederates.

An undated cartoon highlighting the position of black voters in the South. The implication is that this voter evaded the KKK and other terrorist groups, only to find himself forced to vote Democratic at the last minute.

South in the late 1860s and early 1870s, frightening, beating, and even murdering people. In one Louisiana town in 1873, the KKK lynched 50 blacks and two whites after a disputed election. Although Congress took action against the KKK, the damage had been done. Fewer blacks came out to vote when elections were held. White supporters were similarly silenced. Control of the southern state governments fell to the Democratic party.

Most of the old Radical Republican leaders in Congress who had been devoted to the cause of civil rights for blacks had retired or died by the mid-1870s. The priorities of the new leadership were keeping control of Congress and finally ending the bitter sectional conflict between North and South so that the country's economic development could proceed. If this meant abandoning the effort to help the freed slaves in the South, so be it.

By the mid-1870s, northern enthusiasm and energy for reforming the South was weakening as the idealism stimulated by the Civil War began to fade. Other concerns, such as the scandals of the Grant administration and the depression of 1873, were preoccupying voters and politicians alike.

President Grant meant well, but he was not an effective leader. The Fifteenth Amendment and civil rights laws, which required all southern states to allow blacks to vote, were interpreted in such a way by the Supreme Court that they became useless for protecting the rights of blacks. By 1877, all of the former Confederate states except South Carolina, Florida, and Louisiana were once again controlled by whites who had no interest in civil rights for blacks.

In 1877, the Republican Rutherford B. Hayes was finally confirmed as the new President of the United States. A special electoral commission had to be appointed to determine the winner of the election, and Hayes finally triumphed by only one electoral college vote. During the dispute over the election results, Republican leaders promised to remove the last federal troops from southern states if Hayes won the election. Hayes' victory marked the end of the Reconstruction period, and the millions of blacks in the South were left largely defenseless.

THE ERA OF JIM CROW

The South now became a one-party region. Various political and economic groups of whites struggled either to replace the Democratic party or to gain power within it. For a time, rival white factions used African American votes as weapons in their competition. Corruption was widespread since votes were bought and sold. Political and economic competition among whites eventually resulted in further degradation of blacks. Whites could always agree on one thing — their superiority to blacks. "The lowest white man counts for more than the highest Negro" was the widely held attitude.

During the 1890s, the southern states began to design voting regulations that would prevent African Americans from voting. Mississippi was the first state to introduce these new regulations. Each voter was required to a pay poll tax, which blacks could not afford. Voting districts were drawn in such a way that the value of blacks' votes was minimized. Voters were required to take literacy tests and also to demonstrate that they owned property. These requirements were imposed and interpreted in such a way that African Americans were often disqualified from voting. If a potential voter could demonstrate that his grandfather had voted, he was exempt from these requirements.

The "grandfather clause" successfully excluded African Americans from the voting system. Their grandfathers were slaves, and they never had the vote.

Gradually, in the late 1800s and early 1900s, southern states created a racially segregated society, where blacks were kept apart from whites, and whites were clearly supreme. This state of affairs was called Jim Crow, a term derived from a song and dance routine in an old minstrel show. Blacks were often already prevented from voting by the impossible voting requirements and by intimidation. Now, state after state passed laws that placed them in an unequal and subordinate position in all major aspects of life. Schools, churches, playgrounds, restaurants, hospitals, cemeteries, and public transportation were all segregated. The facilities for blacks were almost always inferior. In some places, courts even had separate Bibles for blacks to swear on. Social customs also reflected the notion of black inferiority. As had been the custom during slavery, blacks were expected to behave meekly around whites, always addressing them respectfully. Whites, on the other hand, could speak to a black person of any age as "boy" or "girl."

In the North, conditions were better but far from ideal. In some places blacks were allowed to vote freely. However, northerners were generally unwilling to give African Americans the vote, unless they could be sure that they would vote the "right" way. Many northern communities had laws prohibiting discrimination in public facilities, but these laws were not always enforced and discrimination was common. The courts of the United States did nothing to block these developments. In the 1896 *Plessy v. Ferguson* decision, the Supreme Court confirmed that segregation did not violate the Fourteenth Amendment as long as the "separate facilities were *equal*." Of course, they hardly ever were.

Racism was the norm. Scientific opinion agreed that African Americans were an inferior race. More crudely, Benjamin Tillman of South Carolina, first a governor then a senator, said that African Americans were "an ignorant and debased and debauched race." Violence against African Americans became a part of southern life. One form was lynching: a mob would seize a person thought guilty of a crime and hang him without trial. More than 7,500 blacks were lynched between 1884 and 1914. Many of them had committed no real crime.

If one race be inferior to the other socially, the Constitution of the United States cannot put them upon the same plane.

U.S. Supreme Court, Plessy v. Ferguson, 1896.

BOOKER T. WASHINGTON

Faced with these conditions, blacks responded in different ways. In dozens of cities in the South, they protested against segregated transportation unsuccessfully. Some blacks suggested returning to Africa, an idea that would recur in later years. Booker T. Washington, an outstanding black leader of the time, had a different approach. Born a slave in 1856, Washington urged blacks not to waste their energies protesting inequality. Instead, he said that they should educate themselves to be more efficient workers. Although the work he referred to was agricultural and manual, he believed that this was the way that they could eventually win more equal treatment. The white community played up Washington's ideas. Some blacks thought that he was too accommodating to injustice and prejudice. Their response to Booker T. Washington's stance can be seen as one of the principal causes of the modern civil rights movement.

I would say, "Cast down your bucket where you are". . . . No race can prosper till it learns that there is as much dignity in tilling a field as in writing a poem. It is at the bottom of life we must begin, and not at the top. Nor should we permit our grievances to overshadow our opportunities . . . . The agitation of questions of social equality is the extremist folly.

Booker T. Washington, Atlanta speech, 1895.

Booker T. Washington (1856-1915) opened his own school called the Tuskegee Institute in rural Alabama. The institute was famous for its vocational courses. He also owned many African American newspapers and founded the National Negro Business League. The League, founded in 1900, offered support and advice to black businesses.

THE MOVEMENT IS BORN

Booker T. Washington offered one response to the failure of Reconstruction and the second-class citizenship that black people suffered under Jim Crow. However, it was an entirely different response that led to the beginnings of the civil rights movement. The new movement, which slowly gathered strength, was also influenced by economic and political developments.

THE NIAGARA MOVEMENT

W.E.B. Du Bois was a sociologist. Born in Massachusetts in 1868, he became the first black person to earn a doctorate from Harvard University. He and a number of other young, well-educated blacks strongly disagreed with Booker T. Washington's belief that African Americans should receive an education only so that they could get jobs. He believed that education should not simply teach people to work, it should teach them to live.

In July 1905, a group of blacks led by Du Bois and William Monroe Trotter, a newspaper editor, held a meeting in Canada, just across the American border at Niagara Falls. The meeting took place in Canada because no hotel on the American side of the border would accept blacks. The group, which became known as the Niagara Movement, issued a statement drafted by Du Bois. It called for full civil rights for blacks and urged them to make their demands proudly. The Niagara Movement, starved for funds and opposed by Booker T. Washington, soon broke up, but many of its members then joined what became a more successful organization.

Concerned whites as well as African Americans, such as Du Bois and Trotter, were appalled by a number of vicious race riots that occurred in both the North and South in the early 1900s. These riots were typically set off by a false or exaggerated report of a black

We refuse to allow the impression to remain that the Negro-American assents to inferiority, is submissive under oppression and apologetic before insults. Through helplessness we may submit, but the voice of protest of ten million Americans must never cease to assail the ears of their fellows, so long as America is unjust.

W.E.B. Du Bois, The Niagara Movement, Declaration of Principles, *1905.*

man committing violence against a white. A mob of enraged whites would then try to seize the supposed criminal, and soon blacks and whites would be fighting each other in the streets.

THE NAACP

In August 1908, a race riot occurred in Springfield, Illinois. In the course of the riot, two blacks — one an 84-year-old man — were lynched by a mob less than two miles (3km) from the grave of Abraham Lincoln. News of the riot led a number of progressive whites concerned with the race problem to call for a meeting to discuss the "present evils, the voicing of protests, and the renewal of the struggle for civil and political liberty." Among those issuing the call were Mary White Ovington and Oswald Garrison Villard, both descendants of abolitionists. The meeting in 1909 was attended both by sympathetic whites and by blacks from the Niagara Movement. After further meetings, in 1910 the group launched a new organization, the National Association for the Advancement of Colored People (NAACP). Although most of its first leaders were white, Du Bois became the editor of the organization's journal, *The Crisis*. By 1921, the NAACP had

After the end of the Civil War, lynchings became commonplace in America. This picture of 1882 shows an African American being brutally dragged from his house to be lynched by southern racists.

W.E.B. Du Bois' own book, The Souls of Black Folk, *was published in 1903. In it he stressed the importance of education for African Americans. He also upheld the principles of civil equality and the right to vote.*

some 400 branches throughout the United States. It is still active today.

The goal of the NAACP was to obtain equal rights for black people and, in particular, to obtain enforcement of both the Fourteenth and Fifteenth Amendments. It pushed hard for a federal law against lynching. In 1919 in the South alone, 78 blacks were lynched. Some black soldiers were lynched while wearing their uniforms. That year, the NAACP published a book, *Thirty Years of Lynching in the United States, 1889-1918.*

The NAACP's efforts made the lynching issue a national concern. But repeatedly southern members of the United States Senate used the technique of filibuster to prevent the passage of a federal antilynching law. A filibuster is a legislative maneuver by which a senator can prevent action on a measure by speaking or threatening to speak at such great length that no other business can be accomplished.

The NAACP soon decided that filing lawsuits on behalf of blacks' civil rights was the most promising course to follow. This was because the courts were less susceptible to popular racial prejudices. In the first few decades of its existence, it won several cases involving voting and residential discrimination against blacks. However, states and communities that were determined to discriminate continued to find ways to do so. The NAACP's significant victories were still many years away.

In 1911 blacks and whites formed another organization that is still active today, the National Urban League. It concentrated on expanding economic opportunities for blacks. The Urban League assisted blacks who were coming to the cities looking for work and also trained blacks to be social workers. The NAACP and the Urban League led the civil rights movement over the following decades.

Apart from the progress the NAACP made in the courts, the 1920s and 1930s were frustrating years for the civil rights movement. Du Bois had eagerly supported America's entry into World War I in 1917. President Woodrow Wilson had said the war would "make the world safe for democracy." Du Bois believed that by fighting, black soldiers would pave the way for improved conditions for blacks at home after the war. These hopes came to nothing. The period following the war saw more violence, more lynchings, and continued discrimination.

THE GREAT MIGRATION

In the early twentieth century, a huge shift in population, known as the "Great Migration," was under way. Between 1890 and 1920, nearly three-quarters of a million blacks moved from the rural South to the cities of the North in search of a better life. The movement was intensified by the economic boom caused by World War I. In the years from 1914 to 1920, New York's black population grew from 92,000 to 152,000, Chicago's grew from 44,000 to 109,000, and Detroit's from 5,700 to 41,000. The migration continued for many decades and was one of the most significant population shifts of the twentieth century. During the 1920s alone New York's black population doubled.

In the early years, migrants often traveled north by train, sometimes writing on the sides of the carriages "Bound for the Promised Land." Blacks did find jobs up North, working in the manufacturing, shipbuilding, railroad, mining, and meat-packing industries, but their lives were not easy. Their work was hard and poorly paid. Few labor unions, themselves struggling for recognition by employers, would accept blacks as members. Typically, the new arrivals in the cities lived in small, crowded, unhealthy apartments. Even worse, they came up against the racial prejudices of northern whites, with whom they were now competing for jobs and housing. Segregation had long been part of northern society. There was no need here for new laws or black codes, since the purpose for these had long before been accomplished.

The friction between newly-arrived blacks and working-class whites produced terrible race riots in several cities. In East St. Louis, Illinois, in July 1917, a white mob attacked a black neighborhood. The mob burned houses and fired on residents when they tried to escape. As many as 40 blacks died, and thousands

To promote equality of rights and eradicate caste or race prejudice among the citizens of the United States; to advance the interest of colored citizens; to secure for them impartial suffrage; and to increase their opportunities for securing justice in the courts, education for their children, employment according to their ability, and complete equality before the law.

National Association for the Advancement of Colored People Statement of Purpose, 1910.

lost their homes. Two years later, in the middle of a wave of racial incidents all over the country, Chicago suffered 13 days of rioting. It began when a black teenager went for a swim in an area of Lake Michigan usually frequented by whites. Stones were thrown at him, and he drowned. It was reported that he drowned as a result of being hit on the head with a rock. In the rioting that followed, 23 blacks and 15 whites died, and more than 500 were injured. Nationwide, during the summer of 1919, 120 people died in race riots.

MARCUS GARVEY AND THE UNIA

Marcus Garvey (1887-1940). To American blacks who felt excluded from democracy, Garvey was a vision of hope. He would stand before them in his plumed hat and magnificent uniform, shouting "Up! Up, you mighty race."

The difficulties encountered by working-class people in the new black communities in the cities could not be adequately dealt with by the recently created civil rights organizations. These people were attracted by a flamboyant immigrant called Marcus Garvey. Born in Jamaica in 1887, Garvey had founded there the Universal Negro Improvement Association (UNIA). He came to the United States in 1916 and based himself in Harlem, the black community in Manhattan, New York. By 1919, the UNIA had branches in 30 cities.

Garvey appealed to racial pride. He said that "black" stood for strength and beauty and maintained African Americans should be proud of their noble African heritage. He appealed for universal solidarity

between all African Americans. He said that since white people could not help being racist, it was futile for blacks to appeal to whites' idealism and sense of justice. He believed that racial harmony could best be achieved through racial and ethnic separatism. He rejected colonialism and called for a return to "Africa for the Africans."

Denounced by Du Bois and other civil rights leaders as an opportunistic phony, Garvey nevertheless had a huge following. He claimed the UNIA had several million members. While that number was almost certainly an exaggeration, the UNIA probably did have a total membership of around 500,000. Although most of them had no desire to "return" to Africa, they were attracted by the idea of racial separatism. In 1921, Garvey proclaimed himself president of the "Empire of Africa." But his downfall came quickly. In 1923, the federal government accused him of mail fraud in connection with one of his many business ventures, the Black Star Line. This was a steamship company, that he intended to use to transport blacks to Africa. Two years later, he was sentenced to five years in jail, but President Calvin Coolidge paroled and then deported him in 1927. Garvey died in London in 1940.

The UNIA quickly collapsed, having brought no American blacks to Africa. But the idea of black separatism would emerge repeatedly in the black community during times of frustration with conditions and disappointment with the civil rights movement.

The Universal Negro Improvement Association advocates the uniting and blending of all Negroes into one strong healthy race . . . . It believes that the Negro race is as good as any other, and therefore should be as proud of itself as others are . . . . It believes in the social and political physical separation of all people to the extent that they promote their own ideals and civilization.

Marcus Garvey, 1924.

THE DEPRESSION AND THE NEW DEAL

Like most aspects of American life, the civil rights movement was affected by the Great Depression that began in 1929. When the Depression started, more

For many African Americans the Great Depression represented a grueling struggle for survival. This man in Harlem, New York, has made a job for himself collecting waste cardboard. His load, probably the result of a full day's work, would have earned him only a few cents.

than half of America's blacks still lived in the South. Always the last to be hired and first to be fired, blacks in both the cities and the rural areas of the South found that the low-paying jobs they had previously filled were now taken by whites who had lost better jobs. This and the collapse of farm prices caused hundreds of thousands more blacks to move North. But there, too, jobs were scarce. In New York, for example, unemployment among blacks was almost 50 percent. Overall, during the Depression African Americans lost a third of their jobs in industry.

President Franklin D. Roosevelt's efforts to combat the Depression are collectively referred to as the New Deal. The New Deal did not address racial equality. However, it did a lot to help poor blacks, just as it helped poor whites. Some New Deal programs, such as the Civilian Conservation Corps, which built roads and did conservation work, and the National Industrial Recovery Act codes, which tried to regulate working conditions in industry, segregated blacks or ignored them altogether. Roosevelt, fearing he would lose southern support in Congress for New Deal legislation, refused to support proposals for federal laws against lynching and the poll tax.

In other respects, however, African Americans gained during the New Deal. The federal government, spurred by the President's wife, Eleanor Roosevelt, was more sympathetic to blacks' problems than ever before. Blacks began to be accepted in labor unions, notably the Congress of Industrial Organizations, and unions won federal protection during the New Deal. Many blacks were appointed to important positions in New Deal agencies. Never before had so many blacks served in the federal government. Many New Deal programs, such as unemployment insurance and public works projects, helped people generally and therefore helped blacks.

Millions of African Americans, in addition to millions of white Americans, came to believe that President Roosevelt was their friend. This new feeling provoked a political development of very great significance. Until Roosevelt's time, those blacks who could vote, voted overwhelmingly for candidates of the Republican party, the party of Lincoln and emancipation. During the New Deal period, however, a majority of the blacks who voted — most of them new arrivals in northern cities where blacks could vote freely — began to shift from the Republicans to the Democrats. Black votes

soon became vital to the Democrats. Blacks' support of the Democrats and the Democrats' support for civil rights went hand-in-hand and helped to change American life fundamentally both then and in the decades that followed.

BLACKS AND THE SECOND WORLD WAR

Like the Depression, American preparation for and participation in World War II had a significant effect on the civil rights movement. As had happened in World War I, military spending caused a surge in employment that opened up factory jobs for blacks. This led to another million African Americans moving from the South to the Northeast, Midwest, and West. And as before, the blacks were segregated in the lowest-paying jobs. But now they had organizations and leaders to speak up for their interests.

Asa Philip Randolph, the head of a black union called the Brotherhood of Sleeping Car Porters, and Walter White of the NAACP demanded that the government stop refusing jobs to African Americans in the defense industries. When the government failed to respond, Randolph made plans for a summer 1941 march on Washington in which thousands of blacks

Eleanor Roosevelt (1884-1962) is shown here in 1933 chatting with Mary McLeod Bethune, a prominent campaigner for African American civil rights. Mrs. Roosevelt was described as "a woman of tenderness and deep sympathy." She was a valuable unofficial adviser to her husband, President Franklin D. Roosevelt. It was in part due to her influence that Roosevelt finally mandated an end to discrimination in government employment in 1941.

31

When the U.S. entered World War II, A. Philip Randolph (1889–1979) was afraid that the war would be "the graveyard of our civil liberties." He is shown here leading a march of the League of Nonviolent Civil Disobedience Against Military Segregation, an organization that he formed in 1947.

would demand equal rights in defense employment. The Roosevelt administration strongly opposed the proposed march, fearing it would do more harm than good. After meeting with the President, Randolph finally agreed to call off the march when Roosevelt promised to take action.

On June 25, 1941, President Roosevelt issued the first presidential civil rights directive since the Reconstruction period. It prohibited discrimination in both government and defense industries and set up the Fair Employment Practices Committee to monitor the situation. Compliance with the order was not perfect, but progress had been made.

Success in this area was not matched in others. While 700,000 African Americans were serving in the armed forces, the Army was again segregated, as it had been during World War I, although the Navy was not. The nation was once again afflicted with race riots. In 1943, riots occurred in 47 cities. In Detroit, 34 people — 25 of them blacks — were killed during a two-day outburst. This violence between the races while the U.S. was fighting a war for democracy spurred some people to look more closely at the question of civil rights in America.

THE STRUGGLE INTENSIFIES

In the years after 1945, the struggle for civil rights greatly intensified. In part, this was caused by the powerful influence of international affairs. Both World War II and the Cold War gave Americans reason to pay more attention to the plight of African Americans. During World War II, the United States led a worldwide coalition of nations that defeated the undemocratic nations of Germany, Italy, and Japan in a war costing hundreds of thousands of lives. Nazi Germany, in particular, was notorious for its racist philosophy that denied the human rights of whole peoples and relegated them to a subhuman status. When details of the Nazis' murderous treatment of millions of Jews and others became widely known after the war, Americans were horrified.

A few years after World War II ended in 1945, the United States and the Soviet Union began a rivalry known as the Cold War. Each side maintained that its society was superior to the other's. Each tried to win the support of nations around the world, many of them newly independent and with non-white populations. The United States asserted that its functioning democracy, based on the premise that "all men are created equal," was vastly preferable to the Soviet Union's Communist tyranny, which they perceived as trampling on basic human rights. However, it became increasingly hard to ignore the evidence of inequality in America. The United States government was embarrassed in 1955 when India's ambassador to the United States, a dark-skinned man, was told to move when he sat down in the whites-only section of a Houston, Texas, restaurant. Black Americans, who represented about 10 percent of the total population in 1945, were still second-class citizens. It was true that in the cities of the North, where about half the nation's blacks now lived, there was no segregation or discrimination by law. However, this did not mean that the North was without discrimination. There were many other ways of

Looky here America
What you done done
Let things drift
Until the riots come.
. . .

Yet you say we're fightin
for democracy.
Then why don't democracy
Include me?

I ask you this question
Cause I want to know
How long I got to fight

BOTH HITLER —
   AND JIM CROW?

Langston Hughes, 1943.

33

ensuring segregation in society. The practice known as "red-lining" in real estate clearly illustrates the extent of northern prejudice. It was illegal for banks to give mortgages on property that could be seen as a risky investment. It only took one black family to buy a house to label a whole neighborhood as an "unacceptable risk" in the banks' terms. Consequently, it became almost impossible for blacks to get mortgages, regardless of their financial status. The problem was compounded by the fact that white homeowners often fought vigorously to prevent blacks from becoming their neighbors. In part, this was due to fears regarding the sale of their own property. If they did wish to sell their house, the presence of their black neighbors would prevent banks giving a loan to any prospective buyers.

Despite the informal segregation within northern society, two million blacks were now registered to vote in northern cities, a potentially powerful political force. Some even held public office. Blacks generally enjoyed fair treatment in government programs. But in daily life, northern employers, hotels, landlords, restaurants,

Following a Supreme Court decision, blacks in South Carolina were able to vote for the first time since Reconstruction on August 11, 1948. Although no violent incidents occurred, the expressions on the faces of white onlookers are full of disapproval.

and private schools still discriminated against them. Their income, education, housing, and health were inferior to that of the white population.

In the South, under Jim Crow laws, conditions were far worse. State or local law as well as social custom prescribed separate facilities for blacks and whites in virtually every aspect of life. Most churches were either black or white. Blacks went to separate schools at every stage of their education. They sat in separate areas on buses and trains and in waiting rooms. They were kept out of most restaurants and hotels and many parks and swimming pools. Invariably, the black facilities were inferior to those of the white, despite what the Fourteenth Amendment said about "the equal protection of the laws." Despite the equally clear wording of the Fifteenth Amendment, blacks were often prevented from voting throughout the South.

To many thoughtful Americans, white and black, it was high time for the U.S. to start practicing what it preached. That was the message of an influential book published in 1944, *American Dilemma: The Negro Problem and American Democracy*, by the Swedish social scientist Gunnar Myrdal. Significant consequences soon followed.

Except for a small minority enjoying upper or middle class status, the masses of American Negroes, in the rural South and in the segregated slum quarters in southern and northern cities, are destitute . . . . When slavery disappeared, caste remained. Within this framework of adverse tradition the average Negro in every generation has had a most disadvantageous start.

Gunnar Myrdal, An American Dilemma, *1944.*

THE FIGHT AGAINST JIM CROW

A new civil rights organization, the Congress of Racial Equality (CORE), had been founded in Chicago in 1942 by blacks and whites who believed in peaceful protest actions. It directly confronted discrimination. In 1944, CORE shamed several Washington, D.C., restaurants into serving blacks by picketing with signs reading "Are You for Hitler's Way or the American Way? Make Up Your Mind." In 1948, President Harry S Truman issued an order that began the desegregation of the U.S. Army. Truman also proposed a wide-ranging civil rights program to Congress. He called for an antilynching law and an end to segregation in interstate transportation and the workplace. Truman's legislative proposals were blocked in Congress by an alliance of southern Democrats and conservative northern Republicans, but the issue of civil rights was now on the national political agenda.

The world of sports was the scene of an important civil rights victory at about this time. In 1947, Jackie Robinson, a phenomenally talented athlete, became the

There shall be equality of treatment and opportunity for all persons in the armed forces without regard to race, color, religion or national origin.

President Harry S Truman, Executive Order 9981, July 26, 1948.

first black to play for a major league baseball team. Individual black athletes had occasionally achieved general recognition before. The victories of African American track star Jesse Owens in the 1936 Olympics, held in Berlin, Germany, helped show the falseness of Nazi theories about a German "master race." Hitler left the stadium early to avoid having to congratulate Owens. Joe Louis, another African American, became the heavyweight boxing champion in 1937 by defeating James Braddock.

Baseball was America's "national pastime," and, like so many American institutions, it was segregated. Black players, no matter how talented, were forced to play in the separate "Negro leagues" and were largely ignored by mainstream America. In 1947, however, Branch Rickey, the general manager of the Brooklyn Dodgers, broke this barrier by hiring Jackie Robinson to play for his team. For a time, Robinson suffered abuse from some fans and other players, but he courageously persisted. By the 1950s, baseball in addition to professional tennis and basketball had been integrated, and the sports world could serve as a model for the rest of American society.

Meanwhile, the NAACP's strategy of fighting discrimination in the courts, begun years earlier, was beginning to bring results. In the 1930s, the NAACP filed suits demanding that the federal courts actually apply the separate-but-equal principle announced by the Supreme Court in 1896. This approach brought about the desegregation of law and graduate schools in several states when the courts found that equal facilities had not been provided for black students. The NAACP also won a victory on voting rights in 1944. The Supreme Court ruled that it was unconstitutional to bar blacks from voting in a party's primary elections, the elections in which a party's candidates were chosen. In the one-party South, primaries were often the only election that really mattered.

In the field of public education the doctrine of "separate but equal" has no place. Separate educational facilities are inherently unequal. Therefore [the black students have been] deprived of the equal protection of the laws guaranteed by the Fourteenth Amendment.

Supreme Court decision in Brown v. Board of Education, *1954.*

These decisions chipped away at Jim Crow. In 1946 the Supreme Court ruled that states could not segregate interstate buses. In 1948 it went on to rule that there should be no racial discrimination in the housing market. Then, in 1951, Thurgood Marshall, the NAACP's chief lawyer, brought a case that challenged the basis of segregation itself. The suit, on behalf of a black girl, Linda Brown, was against the entire public school system in Topeka, Kansas, a system segregated like many in the South. The NAACP claimed that such segregation generated a sense of inferiority among blacks and thus violated the Fourteenth Amendment. In its historic and unanimous May 17, 1954, *Brown v. Board of Education of Topeka* decision, the Court agreed with the NAACP's position. Later, the reasoning behind the 1954 public school decision would be applied to other areas where the races were segregated by law, such as public parks and public transportation.

THE SCHOOLHOUSE DOOR

The consequences of the famous *Brown* decision were far-reaching, although some were slow in coming. The Supreme Court had made its decision. Now local authorities had to enforce it. In some places, the process took place relatively quickly and smoothly. But in the Deep South, there was trouble. The Ku Klux Klan once again became active and was joined by new groups, such as the White Citizens' Councils, that preached white superiority and vowed resistance to progress on civil rights. Many state and local officials, supported by 90 southern congressmen, proclaimed their resistance to

Thurgood Marshall is shown here (center) standing in front of the Supreme Court building having won the historic Brown v. Board of Education case in 1954. During 23 years of service with the NAACP, Marshall undertook 32 major cases and won 29 of them.

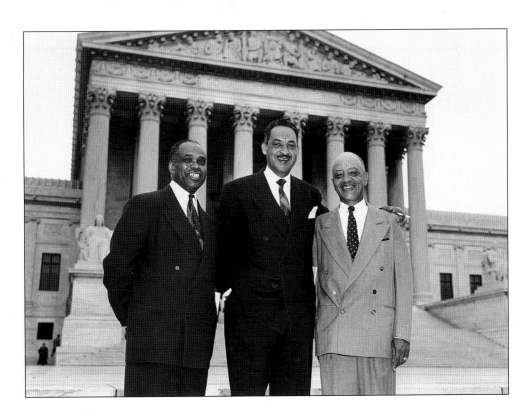

desegregation. They raised the old cry of states' rights, claiming the Supreme Court and federal government had no authority to compel states and localities to change traditional practices. Violent incidents were frequent. When Autherine Lucy, a 26-year-old black woman, tried to enroll in the University of Alabama in 1956, school officials objected, and she was attacked by stone-throwing mobs. She was forced to withdraw.

A major crisis occurred in Little Rock, the capital of Arkansas, in 1957. Arkansas Governor Orval Faubus called up the state's National Guard to prevent the admission of black students to the city's Central High School. President Eisenhower privately doubted the wisdom of the *Brown* decision and said "you cannot change the hearts of people by law." Reluctantly, however, Eisenhower ordered National Guard troops to escort the children to school past mobs of whites who taunted and screamed at them. One morning, a bomb exploded at the home of a 16-year-old black student.

Other communities avoided desegregation by more subtle means. When biracial schools threatened to become a reality, many white parents who could afford to do so withdrew their children from public schools and sent them to private ones. By 1962, eight years after the *Brown* decision, fewer than one-half of one percent of the black children in the Deep South were attending integrated schools. Segregation had been declared unconstitutional, but it still persisted in both North and South. Liberals introduced legislation in Congress to speed up school desegregation and protect civil rights in other areas, but once again southern Democrats and conservative Republicans combined to prevent any significant action. Congress passed weak civil rights legislation in 1957 and 1960 that had little effect.

Resistance continued at southern colleges, too. In the autumn of 1962, President Kennedy had to send U.S. marshals and soldiers to help young James Meredith register at the University of Mississippi over the opposition of Mississippi's governor, Ross Barnett, and crowds of white racists. Two people were killed in the ensuing violence. The next spring, Alabama's Governor George Wallace literally stood in the entrance of the University of Alabama to try to prevent two blacks from enrolling there. He failed, but once again federal troops had to be called in.

On the whole, the North did not have public school systems segregated by law. But housing patterns, with African Americans living in one neighborhood and whites in another, often produced schools that were overwhelmingly attended by one race or the other. The tendency toward segregation in housing was reinforced by the practice of red-lining in the housing market (see page 34).

MARTIN LUTHER KING AND NONVIOLENT PROTEST

The progress of civil rights by means of legal action through the courts was frustratingly slow and difficult to implement. However, the *Brown* decision encouraged southern blacks to take more direct action. They hoped that, if necessary, the courts would back them up. The first test came in Montgomery, Alabama, in late 1955.

Montgomery was the capital of Alabama and known as the "Cradle of the Confederacy." The city was thoroughly segregated. On the city buses African Americans were required to sit in the back. They had to give up their seats to whites when the white seats in the front of the bus were filled. On December 1, 1955, Mrs. Rosa Parks, a black seamstress, was riding home after a hard day's work. She sat in the back as the bus filled up. Feeling very tired, she refused to give up her seat to a white person. She was arrested and fined.

Montgomery's black community had long wanted to do something about the segregated bus system. Many of the community's leaders were clergymen.

When the driver saw that I was still sitting there, he asked me if I was going to stand up. I told him, no, I wasn't. He said, "Well, if you don't stand up, I'm going to have you arrested." I told him to go on and have me arrested.

Rosa Parks.

Mrs. Rosa Parks on her way to jail after refusing to give up her seat on the bus to a white person. Before this incident, Mrs. Parks had already been a member of the Montgomery chapter of the NAACP. She went on to found the Rosa and Raymond Parks Institute for Self-Development in Michigan to help young blacks.

Meeting at a local church, they decided to call on people to stage a boycott. This meant that they would refuse to use the bus service until black passengers ceased to be segregated. A 26-year-old pastor, new to the city, was chosen to lead the boycott. His name was the Reverend Martin Luther King, Jr.

Martin Luther King was born in 1929, in Atlanta, Georgia. He was the son of a Baptist minister. He had earned his doctorate in philosophy from Boston University. In college, King had been greatly impressed by philosophies of nonviolent resistance to evil and by religious thinkers who stressed the responsibility of Christians to fight for social justice. King urged his followers to be ready to suffer, to endure blows, and to be arrested, if necessary, to bring about change for the better. If need be, they would break local laws to claim their rights under the higher laws of the United States Constitution and Christian morality.

The bus boycott lasted one year. Montgomery's African Americans walked to work and organized car pools to avoid using buses. One elderly woman said, "My feet is tired, but my soul is rested." They faced violence from white racists. Terrorists bombed the homes of King and other black leaders and burned black churches. King urged his followers not to respond in kind. "We must love our white brothers no matter what they do to us. We must make them know that we love them." Montgomery's bus company held out until in November 1956, when the Supreme Court declared the city's Jim Crow public transportation laws unconstitutional. On December 21, King and other African Americans boarded a bus, paid the fare, and sat down in the front.

Early in 1957, King, and other clergymen formed the Southern Christian Leadership Conference (SCLC). For several years, SCLC was in the forefront of the fight against segregation and the denial of blacks' right to vote.

SIT-INS AND FREEDOM RIDES

King's nonviolent example helped to inspire the next important development in the civil rights movement. On February 1, 1960, four young students from the black North Carolina Agricultural and Technical College in Greensboro, North Carolina, sat down at the whites-only lunch counter of the town's Woolworth store and said: "coffee, please." The students were

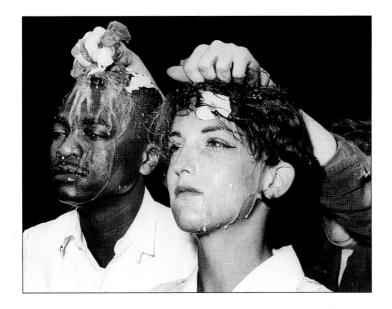

Students attending a workshop in nonviolent demonstration tactics organized by CORE in 1963. This training helped lunch counter demonstrators to remain impassive, despite hostile whites pouring ketchup, mustard, or sugar over them.

refused service. They came back the next day and for days after that. Each day, more students joined them, including, on the fourth day, white students from other colleges. Angry white spectators abused the students with curses, spit, and blows, but the students kept their self-control. As a result of their action, this restaurant and many others throughout the South, were desegregated within six months.

The Greensboro sit-in electrified idealistic people all over America. Elsewhere in the South, African Americans used it to demand equal treatment at restaurants, hotels, libraries, and beaches. In the North, students raised money to support the protesters and organized boycotts of northern Woolworth stores and others that had refused to serve them. In Raleigh, North Carolina, in April 1960, Ella Baker of SCLC and student sit-in leaders formed the Student Nonviolent Coordinating Committee (SNCC) to organize peaceful, interracial protests against discrimination. Although the protestors were committed to nonviolence, many of their actions met with a violent response. "Freedom rides" organized by CORE to integrate interstate bus facilities began in May 1961. The Supreme Court had ruled that bus terminals serving interstate lines should be desegregated, but the ruling had not been implemented. Protestors rode buses through the South and refused to use the segregated rest rooms and restaurants in the terminals. In many places, mobs of whites awaited them. Southern governors refused to take action against the increasingly violent mobs. Riders

We affirm the philosophical or religious ideal of nonviolence as the foundation of our purpose, the presupposition of our faith, and the manner of our action . . . . Love is the central motif of nonviolence . . . . It matches the capacity of evil to inflict suffering with an even more enduring capacity to absorb evil.

SNCC Statement of Purpose, 1960.

An African American passenger points to a segregation sign, due to be removed from all Dallas Transit Company buses the following day, April 26, 1956.

Freedom is never given voluntarily by the oppressor; it must be demanded by the oppressed . . . . Injustice must be exposed, with all the tension its exposure creates, to the light of human conscience and the air of national opinion before it can be cured.

Martin Luther King, Jr.,
Letter from Birmingham Jail, *1963.*

were attacked in Birmingham, Alabama. Federal marshals had to protect them in Montgomery. Finally, in September, the Interstate Commerce Commission ordered an end to segregation on all interstate buses and trains.

Birmingham, a major southern business center, was the scene of a climactic civil rights demonstration in April and May 1963. Martin Luther King and SCLC launched a major drive to desegregate the city's public facilities. Using sit-ins and protest marches, King knew the demonstrators were up against the city's brutal police commissioner, Eugene "Bull" Connor. He expected the confrontation between peaceful demonstrators, who included women and children, and Birmingham's police would gain sympathy for the civil rights movement. Connor turned police dogs and fire hoses against the demonstrators. More than 3,000, including King, were arrested. Writing on scraps of paper with a pen smuggled into his jail cell, King wrote the *Letter from Birmingham Jail*, a stirring discussion of the moral issues involved in the civil rights protests. The televised news with pictures of the confrontation between the police and the demonstrators shocked the nation. President John F. Kennedy said a photo of a huge dog attacking an elderly woman had made him "sick." The national outrage pressured the city's leaders into a comprehensive agreement to desegregate parks, libraries, and other facilities and to employ blacks to work in department stores.

Hundreds of other civil rights demonstrations took place throughout the nation. The events of spring 1963 became a landmark for the U.S. in civil rights.

WE SHALL OVERCOME

The demonstrations led by Martin Luther King and others, and the brutal and often violent response to them of southern officials and mobs, roused the nation's conscience. They caused the United States government to take sweeping action on civil rights in the 1960s. The mid-1960s marked the high tide of the civil rights movement. Some historians have called the period the "Second Reconstruction," a time like that just after the Civil War when the United States government made a determined effort to secure full civil rights for African Americans. In these years, great things were accomplished, although many brave men and women suffered greatly to achieve them.

THE 1964 CIVIL RIGHTS ACT

On June 11, 1963, President Kennedy spoke to the nation on television on the subject of civil rights. He said new laws were needed, although "legislation cannot solve this problem alone. It must be solved in the home of every American." A few days later, Kennedy asked Congress to pass a sweeping civil rights bill to:
• Give the federal government the power to sue in court to desegregate schools.
• Ban discrimination in programs that are federally funded.
• Outlaw discrimination in hotels, motels, stores, gas stations, parks, restaurants, theaters, other places of entertainment, and other public places.
• Outlaw discrimination in employment and establish an Equal Employment Opportunity Commission to enforce the ban.

Despite the moral outcry provoked by recent events, the bill's chances for passage were uncertain. It would give the federal government almost unprecedented authority to act in people's everyday lives. In Congress, conservatives opposed granting the government such power. Many southern senators claimed the new law

We are confronted primarily with a moral issue. It is as old as the Scriptures and is as clear as the American Constitution . . . . Now the time has come for this nation to fulfill its promise. . . . We face a moral crisis as a country and as a people.

President Kennedy, Address to the Nation, June 11, 1963.

would be unconstitutional and violate states' rights. They indicated their willingness to filibuster it to death. One opponent, Senator James Eastland of Mississippi, had earlier pledged to "protect and maintain white supremacy throughout eternity."

Civil rights leaders wanted to put pressure on Congress to pass the bill. They decided to organize a massive summer demonstration in Washington. The Kennedy administration, although sympathetic to the objective, argued against the idea, fearing that if any disorder occurred, the bill's chances of passage would be hurt. This time the organizers were determined to go ahead.

THE MARCH ON WASHINGTON

The March on Washington, formerly called the "March for Jobs and Freedom," was organized primarily by African American leaders. The now elderly A. Philip Randolph, who in 1941 had negotiated with President Roosevelt (see page 32), was assisted by his aide Bayard Rustin. Martin Luther King, Roy Wilkins of the NAACP, James Farmer of CORE, John Lewis of SNCC, and Whitney Young of the Urban League also

The March on Washington was organized to speed up the passage of civil rights legislation. Here, some of the demonstrators are seen cooling their feet in the Reflecting Pool after arriving at the Lincoln Memorial. After listening to speeches by black leaders, they were entertained by performers such as Joan Baez and Bob Dylan.

played prominent roles. Many whites also took part, the majority of them were labor leaders and both Jewish and Christian clergy.

The march took place on August 28, 1963, and turned out to be a tremendous success. Hundreds of thousands of people came to the nation's capital and peacefully marched up to the grand steps of the Lincoln Memorial. Folksingers and show business celebrities entertained the crowd and many people spoke. The throng sang the hymn *We Shall Overcome*. This hymn had become a kind of anthem of the civil rights movement. The highlight was King's great "I Have a Dream" speech (see pages 6-7). Later that day, King and the other leaders met President Kennedy at the White House.

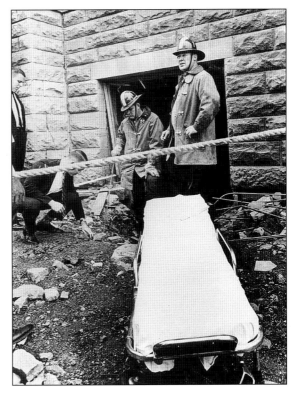

The aftermath of a bomb planted in a Birmingham, Alabama, church. The explosion occurred during Sunday school, killing four black children and injuring 12 others. Here, police and fireman are shown investigating the site, while an empty stretcher awaits one of the victims.

The congressional debate over the civil rights bill was long and bitter. While it went on, there was more violence in the South. In September, a bomb blew up a church in Birmingham, Alabama, killing four black girls. Lyndon B. Johnson became President in November, after Kennedy was assassinated. Johnson made passing the civil rights bill his highest priority. It finally became law on July 2, 1964.

The 1964 Civil Rights Act put the United States government firmly on the side of the civil rights movement. It ended segregation in public facilities and gave the federal government new powers to fight racial discrimination in education and employment. As you will read in the next chapter, American life was profoundly changed as a result of this law.

MISSISSIPPI AND THE RIGHT TO VOTE

Ending segregation was an important civil rights goal. Equally, if not even more important was securing the right to vote for African Americans. Through voting, they could elect public officials who were committed to improving the lives of black people. Blacks in the South still suffered persecution and violence when they tried to vote, and few succeeded. Accordingly, in the 1960s civil rights leaders mounted a campaign throughout the South to register African Americans to vote.

Mississippi, the poorest southern state, was the slowest to change. Violence against blacks was commonplace there. In 1961, a state legislator shot and killed a black man who tried to register to vote. The legislator was acquitted. A black witness to the crime was also killed. On the very night in June 1963 that President Kennedy spoke to the nation about civil rights, Mississippi NAACP leader Medgar Evers was shot in the back and killed, as he was returning home to his wife and children. His murderer was finally convicted almost thirty years later. Blacks in Mississippi, many of them terribly poor and with little or no education, were understandably fearful of asserting their rights.

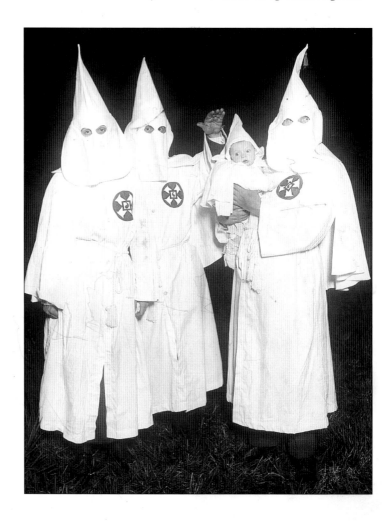

The Ku Klux Klan, which had declined in popularity during the 1920s and early 1930s, resurfaced to oppose the civil rights movement. Its membership consisted largely of "redneck" (rural or working class) white men. These Klan members were photographed at a secret, nighttime meeting.

In the summer of 1964, SNCC and CORE targeted Mississippi for a register-to-vote drive. The project was called "Freedom Summer." Nearly one thousand student volunteers, most of them northern whites, came to Mississippi to help. In addition to registering voters, they ran "freedom schools" to educate black children.

Just as the summer began, yet another tragedy occurred. Two young, northern white volunteers and a Mississippi black had been arrested for speeding while looking into the bombing of a church in Meridian, Mississippi. After their release they disappeared. It turned out that they had been trailed by KKK members and murdered. Their bodies were discovered weeks later.

The summer was a bitter experience for civil rights workers in Mississippi. Fifteen were killed, scores beaten, and hundreds arrested. Only 1,600 black voters were registered in the South. One volunteer later wrote that the summer had been "the longest nightmare I ever had." Some black participants began to question both the value of nonviolence and the usefulness of working with whites. These feelings contributed to the divisions in the civil rights movement that you will read about in the following chapter.

As part of Freedom Summer, civil rights workers also started organizing the biracial Mississippi Freedom Democratic Party (MFDP) to challenge the all-white, pro-segregation Democratic party in the state. At the Democratic Party's National Convention, held in August in Atlantic City, New Jersey, Fannie Lou Hamer argued that a MFDP delegation should be recognized as representing Mississippi and the all-white regular party delegation should be thrown out. The convention refused to do that, but in the future all state delegations to the Democratic Convention were integrated.

THE 1965 VOTING RIGHTS ACT

In early 1965, a drive to register black voters got under way in Selma, Alabama. Selma was a town of 29,000 people. A majority were black, but blacks made up only 3 percent of the eligible voters. The voter registration effort encountered violence, and two civil rights workers were killed. Martin Luther King and SCLC decided to come to Selma. King, who had been awarded

A young black man, his eyes closed against tear gas, supports an unconscious woman after Alabama state troopers broke up the Selma to Montgomery march in 1965.

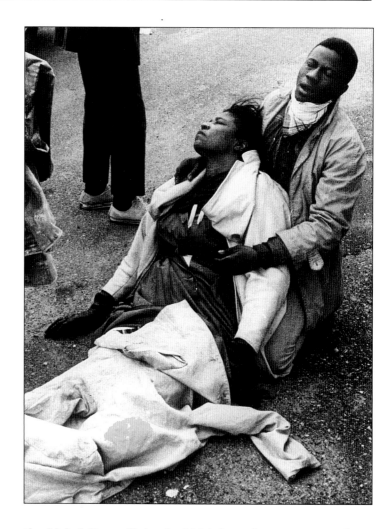

the Nobel Peace Prize in 1964, hoped to attract national attention by leading a march of over 50 miles (80 km) from the town of Selma to Montgomery, Alabama's capital. The march began on Sunday, March 7. Mounted police with tear gas and clubs attacked the marchers, who were forced to retreat to a Selma church. The violence, shown on national television, revolted many Americans, including President Johnson. Saying the violence was "an American tragedy," Johnson called the Alabama National Guard into federal service and ordered it to protect the marchers. A short, symbolic second march took place on March 10. The 300 original marchers were now joined by 50,000 supporters who had come from all over the country.

President Johnson went before Congress on March 15. He urged passage of a bill to give the federal government broad powers to ensure that African Americans could vote freely. Under the new Voting Rights Act, the Department of Justice would be able to supervise voter registration in places where fewer than half the eligible black voters were registered. In a memorable speech, Johnson invoked the great civil rights slogan when he said, "And, we shall overcome." Martin Luther King watched the speech on television. Johnson's words brought tears to his eyes.

On March 21, 1965, the Selma marchers set out again. They reached Montgomery on March 25. After an emotional speech by King, 25,000 people sang *We Shall Overcome*, only this time they modified it to *We Have Overcome*. But that evening, four Ku Klux Klan men followed the car driven by Viola Liuzzo, a white woman from Detroit. She had been driving black marchers back to Selma. The men pulled even with her car, fired into the vehicle, and killed her.

In August 1965, Congress passed the Voting Rights Act of 1965. This act banned the literacy tests that southern states had used to prevent African Americans from voting (see page 21). President Johnson made a moving event of the ceremony at which he signed the law. He invited, in addition to civil rights leaders, Rosa Parks, who had sparked the Montgomery bus boycott nearly ten years earlier, and Vivian Malone, one of the students Governor Wallace had tried to block from entering the University of Alabama in 1963. Renewed several times in later years, the voting rights law had dramatic consequences. In the decade between 1964 and 1975, the number of blacks registered to vote more than doubled for the South as a whole. In some states, such as Mississippi, the increase was of several hundred percent. Large numbers of southern blacks won election to local offices for the first time since Reconstruction.

JOHNSON'S GREAT SOCIETY

President Johnson launched a wide-ranging reform program intended to create in the U.S. what he called the "Great Society." Building on some preliminary plans of President Kennedy, he wanted one part of the Great Society to be "an unconditional War on Poverty." The war on poverty was not specifically a civil rights program. Of the 40 million Americans estimated to be poor in 1960, about 30 million were white. But the 10 million poor blacks represented more than half of all the African Americans in the country. Any plan to end poverty in the U.S. would have to deal with black poverty. The attempt derived much of its spirit from the idealism of the civil rights movement.

At Johnson's urging, Congress created the Office of Economic Opportunity (OEO) in 1964. The OEO managed numerous programs to help poor people. Head Start helped prepare poor preschool children for kindergarten. Upward Bound aimed to help poor teenagers get into college. The Job Corps and the Neighborhood Youth Corps aimed to give young people job training. Volunteers in Service to America (VISTA) aided poor people in both rural and urban areas. The Community Action Program aimed to help poor people participate in the decisions that affected their lives by, for example, giving them access to free legal advice. There were other Great Society initiatives to benefit the poor. Food stamps that could be exchanged for food and welfare benefits for the very poor were increased, as were contributions towards the rent for low-income families. In 1965, a law appropriating federal money for educational aid was passed. This money was used to build libraries, buy textbooks for primary and secondary schools, and for other educational purposes. A new program called Medicaid was also created to provide the poor with medical care.

The War on Poverty had mixed consequences for blacks and for the poor in general. Conservative opponents ridiculed it as a colossal waste of money. On the other hand, many civil rights leaders, who had little part in shaping it, and other supporters thought it did not spend enough money. On average, the OEO spent only $70 a year for each poor person in the United States. The Job Corps accomplished little. Community Action programs failed to reach many of the urban poor. And when they did, poor people sometimes ran up against powerful political interests in city governments that resisted giving them real power. Friction between advocates of change, many of them black, and local politicians was to plague the civil rights movement in coming years.

Many African Americans undoubtedly gained from the housing and education programs as well as the expanded welfare benefits. Head Start clearly helped black children in the cities and continues to help today. On the whole, however, the War on Poverty was simply not big enough to achieve its goal of putting an end to poverty forever.

VIOLENCE AND UNREST

The Civil Rights Act of 1964 and the Voting Rights Act of 1965 were historic achievements that outlawed the most flagrant kinds of discrimination against blacks. But racial discrimination and conflict remained the U.S.'s most serious domestic problem. African Americans insisted on the dismantling of the remaining barriers to their enjoyment of full civil rights and an equal place in American society.

The beatings suffered by civil rights workers in Mississippi in 1964 and by marchers at many demonstrations took their toll. Their experiences and the continuing plight of blacks in U.S. cities caused many young blacks to depart from Martin Luther King's policy of nonviolence. Serious divisions developed within the movement and, simultaneously, the movement lost support in the country as a whole.

RIOTS IN THE CITIES

In the summer of 1965, a terrible riot occurred in Watts, a black area in Los Angeles. The riot was triggered by the action of a policeman who drew his gun

National Guard soldiers help out the fire service by using hoses. Hundreds of blazes were started during the 1965 riot in the Watts area of Los Angeles. Thirty-four people died, and damage, caused largely by fire, totaled $200 million.

while attempting to arrest a young black for reckless driving. The riot lasted for six days, 34 people were killed, thousands arrested, and millions of dollars' worth of property was destroyed. About 15,000 National Guardsmen were called in to assist the police.

Over several consecutive summers, riots in black neighborhoods broke out in Chicago and several other northern cities. Earlier race riots in the U.S. had typically started with attacks by whites against blacks. The riots of the 1960s were different. The violence was mainly between blacks and local police, whites tended to stay away. During the course of the riots, blacks burned down their own neighborhoods. What were the causes of this violence?

The African American population of the cities had increased enormously. Compare these population numbers for several large cities:

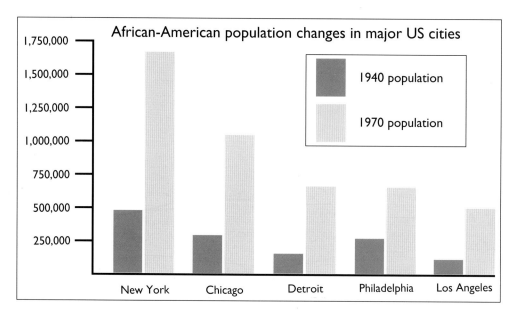

Blacks experienced wretched conditions in these cities. They lived in crowded, crime-ridden areas called ghettos. Their housing, often owned by whites, was both expensive and run-down. The neighborhood schools were similarly run-down and were starved of money and equipment by the city authorities. Poorly educated, many blacks were unable to get good jobs when they could get jobs at all. White-led labor unions in the construction industries, which controlled access to many jobs, often discriminated against them. Unemployment among blacks in 1965 was 8.5 percent, nearly twice the rate for whites. In Watts, Los Angeles, in 1965, it was about 30 percent. Neither the civil rights laws nor the War on Poverty had remedied these conditions.

In 1967, President Johnson appointed the Kerner Commission to study the recent riots. The commission found that, ultimately, "white racism" was responsible for the violence because black inhabitants of the ghettos had lost hope of achieving better lives.

BLACK POWER

The tension in the northern ghettos went hand-in-hand with changes that affected the civil rights movement. Voices favoring black separatism and nationalism gained new strength. Martin Luther King's approach of appealing nonviolently to the conscience of white American society lost its appeal to some younger black activists.

During the 1920s (see page 28), Marcus Garvey had urged blacks to abandon hopes of achieving equality in the United States and to go to Africa. Garvey's plan failed. In 1931, however, Elijah Muhammad founded the Nation of Islam, popularly known as the Black Muslims. They rejected Christianity as a "white man's religion" and said whites were "blue-eyed devils."

What white Americans have never fully understood — but what the Negro can never forget — is that white society is deeply implicated in the ghetto. White institutions created it, white institutions maintain it, and white society condones it . . . . Our nation is moving toward two societies, one black, one white — separate and unequal.

Kerner Commission Report, 1968.

Black Muslims picketing the Criminal Courts building in New York in 1963. Two of their members were standing trial at the time.

Black Panther posters like this began to attract many urban blacks by the mid-sixties. The movement was originally formed to protect African Americans from police harassment.

POWER TO THE PEOPLE

Since we cannot get along with [whites] in peace and equality, after giving them 400 years of our sweat and blood and receiving in return some of the worst treatment human beings have ever experienced, we believe our contributions to this land and the suffering forced upon us by white Americans, justifies our demand for complete separation in a state or territory of our own.

Elijah Muhammad, 1965.

Elijah said, "There are many of my poor black ignorant brothers...preaching the ignorant and lying stuff that you should love your enemy. What fool can love his enemy?" The Muslims favored separation of the races and wanted a part of the United States set aside for African Americans. Appealing to urban African Americans and those in prison populations, too, the Black Muslims urged them to take control of their own lives and be proud of themselves. By the 1960s, the Black Muslims had thousands of members.

Malcolm X was Elijah Muhammad's most significant follower. Born Malcolm Little, he was the son of a Baptist minister who had worked for Garvey. Malcolm lived the life of a small-time criminal until he was arrested for stealing in 1946 at the age of 21. While in prison, he converted to Islam. Released in 1952, Malcolm became a highly effective speaker. He asserted that blacks should not rule out using violence to defend themselves. He mocked the 1963 March on Washington as the "Farce on Washington."

In 1964, Malcolm split with Elijah Muhammad and founded his own group, the Organization of Afro-American Unity. He began speaking of the need for "brotherhood" and reaching out to different groups. But Malcolm was assassinated on February 21, 1965, presumably by followers of Elijah Muhammad. His book, *The Autobiography of Malcolm X*, was published after his death, and it powerfully influenced many young blacks.

An even more radical group was the Black Panthers. They were founded in Oakland, California, in 1966 by two college students, Bobby Seale and Huey Newton. The Black Panthers talked about armed revolt and wore military clothes. At times, they openly carried guns. Over the following years, the Black Panthers attracted much media attention and engaged in several violent confrontations with the police.

Ideas of black separatism and a refusal to reject violence began to be taken up by individuals in the established civil rights organizations. While demonstrating in Mississippi in 1966, Stokely Carmichael, the chairman of SNCC, began to chant "We want black power! Black power!" The slogan alarmed older leaders like Roy Wilkins of the NAACP. It also antagonized

Don't you run around here trying to make friends with somebody who's depriving you of your rights. They're not your friends, no, they're your enemies. Treat them like that and fight them, and you'll get your freedom; and after you get your freedom your enemy will respect you.

Malcolm X, 1964.

Having coined the concept of "Black Power," Stokely Carmichael denied that it would promote racial hatred. He believed that it was "a means to bring Black Americans into the covenant of brotherhood . . . ."

Riots in Chicago broke out only days after Martin Luther King led marches through the city demanding better housing for the poor. The National Guard, shown here encircling a rioter, were called in after three days of looting and burning.

many white liberals who had supported and financed the civil rights movement. Concerns increased when some black leaders made anti-Semitic remarks which appalled many Jews who had been deeply committed to the civil rights movement.

The "black power" call was enthusiastically taken up by young blacks. SNCC and CORE decided that only blacks could hold leadership positions in their organizations. Carmichael's successor as SNCC chairman, H. Rap Brown, remarked that violence was "as American as cherry pie." Brown urged blacks in a Maryland town that had been the scene of racist demonstrations to "burn this town down." Speaking of the white man, Brown said, "Don't love him to death. Shoot him to death." Martin Luther King, however, held to his faith in nonviolence.

THE STRUGGLE AGAINST SEGREGATION

The riots in northern cities and the increasing militance of blacks caused the civil rights movement to focus more on problems in the North. Here, segregation by law — referred to by the Latin term *de jure* segregation — had largely been ended by federal legislation. Now the struggle began against segregation by custom and in fact — *de facto* segregation.

In most of the U.S., blacks lived in separate neighborhoods, even in the North where laws supposedly prevented housing discrimination. African American families wishing to move into a white neighborhood would get no assistance from real estate agents (see page 34). Banks would refuse them loans to buy a home, and insurance companies would not issue them home insurance.

King and SCLC targeted Chicago in 1966 for a campaign against housing discrimination. As they led protest marches in white neighborhoods, they encountered bitter opposition. King and other marchers were hit by stones. Whites in Chicago and elsewhere feared that their neighborhoods would decline, and that crime would increase if blacks moved in. They resented what they saw as favoritism shown by the government to African Americans. This phenomenon, known as "white backlash," seriously weakened the civil rights movement over the following years. In cities such as Chicago political and business leaders did accept the principle of ending housing discrimination. However, in the end King's campaign accomplished little in terms of ending these entrenched discriminatory practices.

King began to believe that the struggle for black civil rights was closely tied to the larger question of poverty in the U.S. In 1967, he developed the idea of a Poor People's Campaign that aimed to pressure the federal government into putting new energy into the fight against poverty, and to persuade corporations to train and hire more poor workers. SCLC's organizers planned to hold massive demonstrations in the summer of 1968 in front of a government building in Washington, D.C.

By this time, the Vietnam War was absorbing much of the nation's attention. The government had little money to spend on new programs. Moreover, just as the Vietnam War divided the nation, it divided the civil rights movement. After some hesitation, many of the more militant black leaders denounced the war and President Johnson for fighting it. Others, such as the leaders of the Urban League and the NAACP, refused to criticize the government's war policy. King came out against the war. He felt it was morally unjustified and was using up resources that would be better spent at home.

Are there no poor whites? But the Negroes get all the antipoverty money . . . . The whites are the majority. You know how many of them come to me, night after night, because they can't get a job? They've been told, we have to hire Negroes first.

Anthony Imperiale, Italian American community leader in Newark, New Jersey, 1968.

THE DEATH OF MARTIN LUTHER KING, JR.

On April 4, 1968, King was shot and killed in Memphis, Tennessee. He was only 39 years old. The murderer was James Earl Ray, a white with a long criminal record. Whether Ray acted alone or as part of a conspiracy is still debated. As news of the tragedy spread through the nation, riots broke out in hundreds of cities. Fires burned in black neighborhoods within sight of the United States Capitol building in Washington. Six days after King's murder, Congress passed a law intended to prevent discrimination in housing. The measure, however, was weak and proved to be ineffective.

The Reverend Ralph Abernathy succeeded King as the head of SCLC. Abernathy attempted to proceed with the Poor People's Campaign. As planned, African Americans, Mexican Americans, and white students camped on the Mall in Washington. But the campaign failed. Rain turned the area into a swamp, violence broke out among the participants, and Congress did its best to ignore the whole thing.

THE FUTURE OF THE CIVIL RIGHTS MOVEMENT

With the Vietnam War at its height and ghetto riots convulsing the cities, 1968 was a turbulent and tragic year in American history. Two months after King's violent death, Senator Robert F. Kennedy, a brother of former President John F. Kennedy, was also assassinated. Robert Kennedy had been an opponent of the war, an ally of the civil rights movement, and a presidential candidate. Anti-war protests and the police's violent response made a shambles of the Democratic National Convention in Chicago that summer.

In the fall election, Richard M. Nixon, the Republican candidate, was elected President. Nixon defeated Hubert H. Humphrey, the Democratic candidate. Humphrey was both a firm supporter of civil rights and, as Johnson's vice president, closely tied to the Vietnam War. Governor George C. Wallace of Alabama, the former defender of segregation, also ran and received nearly ten million votes.

Richard Nixon used what was called a "Southern Strategy" in his campaign. He let it be known that if elected, he would not press hard for desegregation of southern schools. Taking advantage of white backlash, he carefully crafted his campaign to appeal to whites, northern and southern, who either had no sympathy for the civil rights movement or had lost what sympathy they formerly had. Nixon knew the "silent majority" of Americans was tired of unrest in the streets, protests, and demonstrations. He pledged to restore "law and order."

It is sometimes said that 1968 was the end of the civil rights movement. Martin Luther King was dead. The remaining leaders disagreed among themselves. The nation's political system no longer responded to the movement's appeals as it had earlier in the decade. But the struggle for equality by African Americans, which is what the civil rights movement was fundamentally about, continued beyond 1968, and it still continues today.

BUSING AND AFFIRMATIVE ACTION

Since 1968, there have been two approaches to remedying racial discrimination: school busing and affirmative action. Both have provoked intense controversy. After

Martin Luther King was buried in Atlanta, Georgia, after a nationally televised funeral march through the city. Thousands of mourners formed a procession behind the coffin, which was transported on a mule-drawn wagon.

the Supreme Court's historic 1954 decision declaring segregated schools unconstitutional, southern school districts devised many schemes to avoid desegregation. In 1969, the Supreme Court finally declared that segregation must end "at once." Lower federal courts began implementing school busing plans to transport children of one race to schools previously attended only by children of the other race.

Although buses had taken America's children to school for decades, their use in integrating public schools caused an uproar in both the North and the South. President Nixon denounced court-ordered busing. In later years, President Gerald Ford and President Ronald Reagan also expressed their disapproval of it. When a busing plan went into effect in Boston in 1974, serious disorders followed. Black students were hit with stones, and white students were stabbed by blacks. In Boston and other cities, as previously in the South, whites who could afford to do so started sending their children to private schools, leaving the city schools overwhelmingly black. In 1974, the Supreme Court, in a case concerning a busing plan for Detroit and its

Policemen protect the route as school buses carrying black students travel toward South Boston High School. When the busing plan went into effect, many whites boycotted the desegregated schools.

suburbs, changed course and sharply limited lower courts' authority to order busing. This order is still operative today.

Affirmative action is the general term for a wide variety of programs intended to expand educational and employment opportunities for African Americans, other minorities, and women. It has been the source of great controversy — even civil rights supporters cannot agree about the validity of affirmative action. The idea first originated in the Kennedy and Johnson administrations of the early 1960s. Since then, the federal government and some state governments have encouraged businesses and professional institutions, such as law and medical schools, to make special efforts to train, hire, and admit blacks. Governments seek out black-owned firms when awarding contracts. In some cases, corporations and institutions have set specific numerical quotas, or targets, for hiring or admitting blacks. This means that in some instances, African Americans are given jobs even though they may appear to be less qualified than rejected white applicants.

Defenders of these procedures insist they are necessary to make up for the discrimination suffered by blacks for hundreds of years. Opponents — and some of the unsuccessful white applicants — claim that they amount to reverse discrimination: African Americans are unjustly favored solely because of their race. The issue is a very complicated one. In part, this is because so many different kinds of affirmative action programs exist. The issue has divided civil rights supporters. Some blacks have strongly opposed affirmative action programs that use quotas. They argue that the blacks who benefit would be thought to be unable to succeed on their own.

The Supreme Court has been wrestling with affirmative action cases since 1977. In the 1996 presidential election, Republican candidate Bob Dole criticized affirmative action, while President Bill Clinton supported the concept. That year, California voters approved a measure to forbid race-based preferences in state programs. This measure was later ruled unconstitutional by a California state court. Then the U.S. Court of Appeals overruled this and permitted the law to go into effect. The case went to the Supreme Court, which refused to block its enforcement. The Court may decide to review the previous lower court's ruling. Affirmative action remains a major civil rights issue for the nation to resolve.

You do not take a person who for years has been hobbled by chains, liberate him, bring him up to the starting line of a race, and then say, "You are free to compete with all the others," and still justly believe that you have been completely fair. Thus, it is not enough just to open the gates of opportunity; all our citizens must have the ability to walk through those gates.

President Lyndon B. Johnson, 1965.

ENDURING PROBLEMS

The civil rights movement brought impressive gains for black Americans. The elimination of Jim Crow discrimination (see page 21), the opportunity to pursue careers in the worlds of politics, business, the arts, entertainment, and sports, the ability to vote and participate meaningfully in public life — these were all tremendously important achievements. In a fundamental sense, however, the work of the civil rights movement must still be considered incomplete.

Civil rights activists aspired to more than the elimination of discriminatory laws and practices. They aimed to make black Americans first-class citizens, the equal of their white brothers and sisters in every respect. Let us look back at some of the key statements in the history of the movement. In its 1910 Statement of Purpose, the National Association for the Advancement of Colored People said its goal was the elimination of "race prejudice among the citizens of the United States." Fifty-three years later, the Reverend Martin Luther King, Jr., dreamed of the day when his children would "live in a nation where they will not be judged by the color of their skin but by the content of their character." In 1965, President Johnson said, "It is all of us who must overcome the crippling legacy of bigotry and injustice."

Sadly, the happy day when the United States will have "overcome" has not yet arrived. More than a hundred years after the abolition of slavery, black Americans still do not live as well as whites. Wherever we look, we find clear evidence of this.

We get thousands of calls a year from black employees telling us about problems related to discrimination in hiring, promotion, job assignments, and sometimes racial epithets in the workplace.

Ted Shaw, NAACP Legal Defense and Education Fund, 1996.

THE PERSISTENCE OF DISCRIMINATION

The presence of token blacks in managerial positions has done little to resolve the problem of continuing discrimination in the business world. In 1996, a shocking instance became the subject of headlines. The Texaco company had been sued for employment discrimination

by several black employees. Top company executives — all of them white — discussed the case at a meeting. They considered destroying incriminating documents and made derogatory remarks about the black employees. Unknown to the other participants, one executive had taped the meeting and made the tape public. Eventually, the company settled the suit for $140 million, the largest settlement ever made in an employment discrimination case.

Churches and social clubs are typically white or black. All-white private schools for the children of well-off white families are common. Racial violence directed against blacks persists as well. Happily, hate groups, such as the KKK, appear now to be in serious decline, thanks in part to a determined effort begun in the mid-1960s by the Federal Bureau of Investigation and other law-enforcement authorities. But violent incidents of whites beating blacks still occur. In Howard Beach, New York, in 1986, a group of white teenagers attacked with baseball bats a few blacks who had "invaded" their neighborhood.

Every year, it seems, a controversial incident occurs involving the use of violence by white police against black people. On March 3, 1991, Los Angeles police stopped a car driven by a black man, Rodney King. A videotape made by a bystander showed that the police

Los Angeles police aim their guns at a suspect during two days of rioting that followed the acquittals of four officers in the Rodney King case in April 1992. During the riots, more than 1,500 people were injured, many of them critically.

were excessively violent when they arrested King. A year later, four of the officers were brought to trial. Despite the evidence of the tape, the largely white jury acquitted them in April 1992. The news of the verdict caused the black areas of Los Angeles to explode. Dozens of people were killed in the worst rioting since the 1960s. Months later, the police were tried again for violating King's civil rights, and two of the four were convicted.

THE INNER CITIES

The homeless population of the inner cities reached alarming levels in the 1980s and 1990s. This man has made a shelter for himself out of plywood boards and scraps of carpet.

The 1992 Los Angeles riots point to the most serious problem facing African Americans and the nation as a whole today: the terrible condition of the black ghettos in the inner cities. Several factors account for the steady decline in conditions in these urban areas. Changes in the national and even the international economy have contributed to the worsening situation. Unskilled factory work had been the primary source of employment for inner-city residents. In recent years, however, those jobs have largely disappeared. The

result in some places has been inner-city unemployment levels as high as 60 percent.

The federal government has not made inner-city problems a priority. President Johnson's attempt to end poverty failed. However, no President since Johnson left office in 1969 has even tried to do as much about the inner cities.

The diminished power of the civil rights movement since the late sixties has drawn attention away from urban problems. Ironically, the positive results of the civil rights movement have also contributed to the decline of black neighborhoods. As opportunities for blacks opened up in the larger society, some inner-city residents who were educated and possessed skills needed by the economy were able to move to better neighborhoods. Those who remained were the least productive segment of the population, the people least able to take care of themselves.

These factors have combined to create an urban underclass — a group of people in the inner city, many of them black, who are terribly poor and have no way to escape poverty. For many in this underclass, poverty has been their families' way of life for generations. They suffer all the worst ills of modern society to a greater degree than any other portion of the population: high rates of unemployment, truancy, violence, crime, drug addiction, and family breakdown.

Many of the underclass survive only thanks to welfare checks and other benefits provided by the government. In 1996, the U.S. government sharply cut back on its funding for welfare and tightened the regulations governing who is eligible for benefits. Opponents of these changes predict that they will be disastrous for hundreds of thousands of inner-city residents.

THE PERSISTENCE OF BLACK SEPARATISM

Wretched conditions in the inner cities have increased the appeal of black separatists. These are the black leaders who reject the ideal of an integrated United States in which blacks and whites will share equally in prosperity.

In the late 1980s, the Black Muslim leader Louis Farrakhan became an important spokesman for separatism. Like earlier separatist leaders, Farrakhan is extremely controversial. Despite having referred to

The real evil in America is the idea that undergirds the setup of the Western world, and that idea is called white supremacy.
... Now, brothers, moral and spiritual renewal is a necessity. Every one of you must go back home and join some church, synagogue, temple, or mosque that is teaching spiritual and moral uplift .... Black man, you don't have to trash white people. All we got to do is go back home and turn our communities into productive places.

Louis Farrakhan at the Million Man March, October 16, 1995.

Judaism as a "gutter religion" and been associated with bigoted remarks about homosexuals, Catholics, and others, he has a large following in the inner cities. Farrakhan urges blacks to reject crime, drugs, and irresponsibility, lead upright, moral lives, and begin to solve their communities' problems on their own. On October 16, 1995, Farrakhan led a large rally in Washington, D.C., called the Million Man March for "atonement and reconciliation." Hundreds of thousands of African American men heard Farrakhan exhort them to take care of themselves, their families, and their communities.

October 16, 1995. Hundreds of thousands of black men came to the nation's capital to join the Million Man March. The march was led by the controversial Black Muslim leader Louis Farrakhan. It was intended to symbolize the need for blacks, especially black men, to take care of other blacks and not to expect help from the white community.

LASTING ACHIEVEMENTS

The consequences of the civil rights movement, with all its triumphs and tragedies, have transformed the United States. From the baseball field to the U.S. Army, from the classroom to the Supreme Court, the nation has been profoundly changed by the struggle of African Americans for equality. The civil rights movement pressured the federal government into passing laws banning racial discrimination, and this played a tremendous part in bringing about the changes. So did the countless sit-ins, marches, and demonstrations all over the country. The movement insisted on a fundamental truth: a black person is the equal of any other person and is entitled to the same rights and opportunities. As that message began to get across — and it still has not reached all Americans — the lives of African Americans improved.

In 1983, Congress took official notice of the civil rights movement's contributions. It passed a law making January 15, Martin Luther King's birthday, a national holiday. His church in Montgomery, Alabama, is now a national landmark. Montgomery itself renamed a major street the Martin Luther King, Jr., Expressway, and many other cities did the same. The legacy of this outstanding national leader will live on.

THE DISAPPEARANCE OF LEGAL SEGREGATION

The most obvious consequence of the civil rights movement was the disappearance of the Jim Crow society (see page 21) that had prevailed in the South for so long. Although old customs of segregation and black deference to whites linger on in small rural communities, "Whites only" signs no longer hang in restaurants and theaters or at swimming pools and public toilets. Unlike Rosa Parks in 1955, African Americans no

Kids today, they're used to the way things are. Try as you can, you can't believe that white people once treated black people that way. It seems like something that happened long, long ago.

Karyn Reddick, a black student in Selma, Alabama, 1985.

longer have to go to the back of the bus. (See page 42.) Southern workers, whether they work in road construction crews or as white-collar office staff, are integrated.

Many white parents, North and South, have taken their children out of the public schools to avoid integration and sent them to all-white private schools. Nevertheless, by the mid-1970s whites and blacks were sitting in the same classrooms in more than 80 percent of the public schools in the South. The South's record on school desegregation is now better than the North's. The civil rights movement has also opened the doors of America's colleges to black students. The number of African American college students quadrupled during the 1970s.

BLACK OFFICEHOLDERS

General Colin Powell in action at a press conference during the Gulf War of 1990-1991. The first African American to hold the highest military rank in the U.S. armed forces, Chairman of the Joint Chiefs of Staff, Powell became something of a national icon.

Before the successes of the civil rights movement in the 1960s, only a few dozen blacks held elective office. In 1970 there were only about 1,000 black elected officials in the United States. By 1990, however, there were more than 7,000. When Carl Stokes became mayor of Cleveland in 1967, he was the first African American to be elected mayor of a major city. In the following years, blacks were elected mayors of many other large cities. In 1989, Douglas Wilder of Virginia became the first black governor. Black members of Congress formed the Congressional Black Caucus in 1969. It wields considerable power regarding legislation and appointments, particularly when a Democrat is President.

A natural accompaniment to the increasing power of the African American vote has been the increasing number of blacks appointed to important positions in government. President Johnson appointed the first black Cabinet officer, Robert Weaver, as Secretary of the Department of Housing and Urban Development in 1966. Since then, blacks have served in every President's Cabinet. At the time when President George Bush chose

General Colin Powell to be the Chairman of the Joint Chiefs of Staff in 1989, he put a black in the nation's highest military post.

AMERICA'S POLITICAL PARTNERS

Another consequence of the civil rights movement was a change in voting patterns in the United States. During Reconstruction, blacks voted overwhelmingly for the Republican party, the party of Abraham Lincoln. Since the New Deal period of the 1930s, however, blacks have increasingly voted for Democratic candidates. At that time many southerners who were committed to segregation held power within the Democratic party. Nevertheless, since the New Deal era, the national Democratic party has been more willing than the Republicans to use the resources of government on behalf of blacks. This tendency became more pronounced during the 1960s, in the heyday of the civil rights movement, and it continues today. In consequence, blacks have become probably the most solidly Democratic voting group in the country.

Black votes probably made a difference in the close elections of 1960 and 1976 when, respectively, Democrats John Kennedy and Jimmy Carter were elected President. In 1984 and 1988, Jesse Jackson, another former colleague of King, made a determined effort to win the Democratic nomination for President. Jackson talked of a "rainbow coalition" that would unite people of diverse races and ethnic groups in a movement for justice and economic opportunity. He did not succeed in winning the nomination, but he became a powerful force within the Democratic party.

In recent years, Republicans have tried to improve their standing among African Americans. Their efforts received a considerable boost when General Powell, after retiring as Chairman of the Joint Chiefs of Staff, let it be known that he was a Republican. Powell was immensely well-regarded among all segments of the American population and gave serious thought to trying for the Republican presidential nomination in 1996. He eventually decided not to run, but the option remains open to him in the future.

It is no longer an unrealistic fantasy to imagine a black person being elected President of the United States. Such a prospect would have been impossible without the civil rights movement.

ECONOMIC PROGRESS

As a consequence of the civil rights movement, African Americans benefit from better education and less discrimination. Economic data show that more blacks than ever before are enjoying economic success and entering the middle class of U.S. society. In the mid-1990s, the United States Census Bureau reported that the poverty rate for blacks had fallen below 30 percent. This was the first time that this had ever happened. This development is highly welcome, but we must remember that large numbers of African Americans remain trapped in poverty, as you read in the previous chapter.

Before the 1960s, economically successful African Americans were few and far between. Today, thanks in part to affirmative action, blacks work as bankers, publishers, financial consultants, managers, public officials, and at a host of other occupations. In 1983, Lieutenant Colonel Guion S. Bluford, Jr., became the first black astronaut. African Americans are still underrepresented, however, at some of the highest levels of American business, where a phenomenon called tokenism has developed. Companies promote a few blacks to prominent positions as "tokens" of their nondiscriminatory policies, while effective power is still wielded by whites.

THE ARTS, ENTERTAINMENT, AND SPORTS

Sarah Vaughan, an African American singer, was invited to sing at a social gathering in the White House in 1966. After she sang, she danced with President Johnson. Later, friends found her crying in her dressing room, overcome with emotion. She told them that she was overwhelmed by being at the White House in Washington, D.C. Twenty years earlier, she said, she could not have gotten a hotel room in the city.

Today things are very different. Thanks to the civil rights movement, audiences are no longer segregated, and dozens of star performers who are black have careers equal in every respect to those of whites. Wherever one looks, in sports, in symphony orchestras and in rock bands, in films and on theater stages, in advertising and in television commercials, one see blacks and whites performing on apparently equal terms.

Maya Angelou became America's best-known poet when she read her poem On the Pulse of the Morning *at President Clinton's inauguration on January 20, 1993.*

In virtually every sport, black athletes play alongside whites and are stars. In fact, in sports like basketball, black stars may well outnumber white. Despite the success of African Americans in all areas of sports, true equality has not been won in this area. While there are many black football and basketball stars, black quarterbacks and basketball coaches are few. Nor do many blacks hold managerial positions in sports organizations.

A CHALLENGE FOR THE UNITED STATES

The United States was founded in a burst of idealism in 1776. Living up to the ideal of the Declaration of Independence — that "all men are created equal" — remains the United State's greatest challenge. In race relations, very serious and difficult problems persist, especially in the inner cities. Closing the gap between white and black America must be the priority for the country's leaders and, even more importantly, for every citizen.

Fortunately, the enormous gains that blacks have made in recent years with the help of the civil rights movement offers encouragement. In fact, the United State's history shows that time after time, often after enormous sacrifices, the American people in the end do rise to meet the most difficult challenges. With good will and hard work, Americans will yet, as Martin Luther King hoped back in 1963, "lift our nation from the quicksands of racial injustice to the solid rock of brotherhood."

GLOSSARY

abolitionism
The movement begun in the early 1800s to end slavery.

African Americans
The black population of the United States.

Black Codes
Laws passed by southern governments immediately after the Civil War that denied full civil rights to blacks.

boycott
A refusal to do business with an organization in an attempt to pressure it to change its policies.

civil rights
A citizen's rights under the law.

the Confederacy
The country that the 11 southern states attempted to create when they seceded from the United States in 1861.

CORE
Congress of Racial Equality. A civil rights organization founded in 1942.

Constitution
Document written in 1787 to define the powers of the United States government and its relationship to the state governments.

de facto segregation
Segregation maintained by custom.

de jure segregation
Segregation imposed by law.

discrimination
The denial of equal rights or opportunities to people solely because of their ethnic, racial, or religious background.

federal government
The overall government of the United States, as opposed to the governments of the individual states.

ghetto
An area in a city inhabited by a single minority group. In the U.S. the black ghettos are often depressed and crime-ridden neighborhoods.

Jim Crow
Term used to describe the racially segregated society created by law in the South in the late nineteenth century.

lynching
The mob killing of a black who was thought, often without good reason, to have committed a crime.

NAACP
The National Association for the Advancement of Colored People. A civil rights organization, founded in 1909, which supported full equality for blacks.

quotas
Specific numerical targets for employing or admitting members of one particular ethnic, racial, or religious group.

racism
Racial hatred provoked by the belief that one race of people is superior to other races.

Reconstruction

The years after the Civil War, and the attempt during that period to bring the former Confederate states back into the Union and help the newly free blacks.

reverse discrimination

The term used to describe the favoring of minorities over others solely because of their race or gender.

school busing

Transporting students by bus to schools out of their home neighborhoods as a means to end school segregation.

segregation

The separation of whites and blacks, with the implication that blacks are inferior.

separatism

The idea that blacks should not expect help from or cooperate with whites. Some separatists have favored founding a new nation consisting only of blacks from America.

sit-in

A civil rights protest tactic first used in 1960 by demonstrators at restaurants who refused to obey segregation regulations.

SCLC

Southern Christian Leadership Conference. A civil rights organization founded in 1957 and led by Martin Luther King, Jr., until his death in 1968.

SNCC

Student Nonviolent Coordinating Committee. A civil rights organization founded in 1960.

tokenism

The practice by businesses and other organizations of putting a few blacks in publicly prominent positions as proof of their nondiscriminatory policies.

unconstitutional

A practice, regulation, or law that conflicts with the United States Constitution.

underclass

People living in the inner cities who are trapped in poverty and subject to high rates of unemployment, crime, drug abuse, illegitimacy, and other social problems.

Underground Railroad

The network that helped thousands of slaves escape from slavery in the years preceding the Civil War.

Urban League

A civil rights organization founded in 1910.

white backlash

The feeling that developed among some whites in the mid-1960s that the civil rights movement had gone too far.

FURTHER READING

Baldwin, James. *Notes of a Native Son*. Beacon Press, Boston, 1984

Bullard, Sara. *Free At Last: A History of the Civil Rights Movement and Those Who Died in the Struggle*. Oxford University Press, New York, 1993

Carmichael, Stokeley. *Black Power: The Politics of Liberation in America*. Random House, New York, 1967

Dolan, Sean. *Pursuing the Dream: Milestones in Black American History, 1965-1971*. Chelsea House, New York and Philadelphia, 1995

Franklin, John Hope. *Racial Equality in America*. University of Chicago Press, Chicago, 1976

Hamilton, Virginia. *W.E.B. Du Bois: A Biography*. HarperCollins, New York, 1972

Harley, Sally. *A. Philip Randolph: Labor Leader*. Chelsea House, New York and Philadelphia, 1989

Harris, Jacqueline L. *History and Achievement of the NAACP*. Franklin Watts, New York, 1992

Haskins, James. *Freedom Rides: Journey for Justice*. Hyperion, New York, 1995

—— *The Life and Death of Martin Luther King, Jr.*, Morrow, New York, 1992

—— *The March on Washington*. HarperCollins, New York, 1993

Hauser, Pierre. *Great Ambitions: Milestones in Black American History, 1896-1909*. Chelsea House, New York and Philadelphia, 1995

Henry, Christopher E. *Forever Free: Milestones in Black American History, 1863-1875*. Chelsea House, New York and Philadelphia, 1995

Kelley, Robin D.G. *Into the Fire: African Americans since 1970*. Oxford University Press, New York, 1996

Krug, Elisabeth. *Thurgood Marshall: Champion of Civil Rights*. Fawcett Columbine, New York, 1993

Lawler, Mary. *Marcus Garvey: Black Nationalist Leader*. Chelsea House, New York, 1988

Malcolm X. *The Autobiography of Malcolm X*. Ballantine Books, New York, 1973

McKissack, Patricia and Frederick. *The Civil Rights Movement in America from 1865 to the Present*. Children's Press, Chicago, second edition, 1991

Myers, Walter Dean. *Now Is Your Time! The African-American Struggle for Freedom*. HarperCollins, New York, 1991

Powledge, Fred. *We Shall Overcome: Heroes of the Civil Rights Movement.* Scribner's, New York, 1993

Schroeder, Alan. *Booker T. Washington: Educator and Racial Spokesman.* Chelsea House, New York and Philadelphia, 1992

Trotter, Joe William, Jr. *From a Raw Deal to a New Deal: African Americans, 1929-1945.* Oxford University Press, New York, 1996

Tygiel, Jules. *Baseball's Great Experiment: Jackie Robinson and His Legacy.* Oxford University Press, New York, 1983

Weisbrot, Robert. *Marching Toward Freedom: Milestones in Black American History, 1957-1965.* Chelsea House, New York and Philadelphia, 1994

Williams, Juan. *Eyes on the Prize: America's Civil Rights Years 1954-1965.* Viking Press, New York, 1987

TIMELINE

1609 — First blacks are brought to Virginia

1776 — American Declaration of Independence

1787 — Constitution of the United States is written

1861 — Civil War begins

1862 — President Lincoln issues Emancipation Proclamation

1863 — Race riots in northern cities

1865 — Civil War ends
— Thirteenth Amendment ratified

1868 — Fourteenth Amendment ratified

1870 — Fifteenth Amendment ratified

1895 — Booker T. Washington delivers Atlanta speech

1896 — *Plessy v. Ferguson* decision of Supreme Court

1905 — Niagara Movement organized

1909 — NAACP founded

1916 — Marcus Garvey comes to United States

1934 — Elijah Muhammad leads Black Muslims

1941 — President Roosevelt issues order barring discrimination in defense industry

1942 — CORE founded

1948 — President Truman issues order ending segregation in armed forces

1954 — *Brown v. Board of Education* decision of Supreme Court

1955 — Montgomery bus boycott begins

1959 — SCLC founded

1960 — Sit-ins begin
— SNCC founded

1961 — Freedom rides begin

1963 — Demonstrations in Birmingham
— President Kennedy proposes sweeping civil rights bill
— March on Washington

1964 — Civil Rights Act passed
— Freedom Summer; three civil rights workers murdered

1965 — Malcolm X assassinated
— Marches in Selma
— Voting Rights Act passed
— Watts riot; riots in other cities follow in succeeding years
— War on Poverty begins

1966 — Stokely Carmichael calls for "Black Power"
— Robert Weaver appointed Secretary of Housing and Urban Development, first black Cabinet member

1967 — Thurgood Marshall appointed first black Supreme Court justice
— Carl Stokes elected mayor of Cleveland, first black mayor of a major city

1968 — Martin Luther King, Jr., assassinated
— Poor People's Campaign fails

1969 — School busing to achieve integration begins

1974 — Supreme Court limits school busing

1983 — Congress makes Martin Luther King's birthday a national holiday

1984 — Jesse Jackson is candidate for Democratic presidential nomination

1989 — Colin Powell appointed first black Chairman of Joint Chiefs of Staff

1992 — Los Angeles riot following acquittal of police in Rodney King trial

1995 — Louis Farrakhan leads Million Man March

1996 — California voters reject affirmative action

INDEX

Numbers in *italics*
indicate pictures or charts

ACKNOWLEDGMENTS

The publishers are grateful to the following for permission to reproduce photographs:

Cover photo (large): Flip Schulke/Corbis
Cover photo (small): Joseph Schwartz Collection/
                    Corbis
Corbis-Bettmann, pages 6, 11, 20, 25, 28, 29, 31, 32, 34, 37, 39, 41, 42, 45, 46, 48, 51, 53, 55, 56, 58, 60, 63, 64, 66, 68, 71; The Hulton Getty Picture Collection, page 9; Peter Newark's Western Americana, pages 7, 10, 12, 13, 14, 17, 18, 23, 26, 44, 54.